S0-BZK-058

Genealogy Online

Special America Online Edition

Elizabeth Powell Crowe
Bill Mann

McGraw-Hill
New York • San Francisco • Washington, D.C. • Auckland • Bogotá
Caracas • Lisbon • London • Madrid • Mexico City • Milan
Montreal • New Delhi • San Juan • Singapore
Sydney • Tokyo • Toronto

McGraw-Hill

A Division of The **McGraw·Hill** Companies

Copyright © 1998 by The McGraw-Hill Companies, Inc. All rights reserved. Printed in the United States of America. Except as permitted under the United States Copyright Act of 1976, no part of this publication may be reproduced or distributed in any form or by any means, or stored in a data base or retrieval system, without the prior written permission of the publisher.

1 2 3 4 5 6 7 8 9 0   AGM/AGM   9 0 3 2 1 0 9 8

ISBN 0-07-014755-8

The sponsoring editor for this book was Michael Sprague and the production supervisor was Clare Stanley. It was set in Vendome by North Market Street Graphics.

Printed and bound by Quebecor/Martinsburg.

McGraw-Hill books are available at special quantity discounts to use as premiums and sales promotions, or for use in corporate training program. For more information, please write to the Director of Special Sales, McGraw-Hill, 11 West 19th Street, New York, NY 10011. Or contact your local bookstore.

Information contained in their work has been obtained by The McGraw-Hill Companies, Inc. ("McGraw-Hill") from sources believed to be reliable. However, neither McGraw-Hill nor its authors guarantee the accuracy or completeness of any information published herein and neither McGraw-Hill nor its authors shall be responsible for any errors, omissions, or damages arising out of use of this information. This work is published with the understanding that McGraw-Hill and its authors are supplying information but are not attempting to render engineering or other professional services. If such services are required, the assistance of an appropriate professional should be sought.

This book is printed on recycled, acid-free paper containing a minimum of 50% recycled, de-inked fiber.

To my mother, Frances Spencer Powell

This one is for Patti and Jennifer, who put up with my virtual disappearance during this project and did whatever it took to make sure the rest of our lives didn't end while I was MIA.

CONTENTS

Contents

Acknowledgments

As with any book, this one was made possible by the efforts of many people besides the authors. First, we would like to thank every person mentioned and quoted in this edition of the book. Obviously, without all your help, the book would still just be a dream.

Very special thanks to Cliff Manis, Terry Morgan, and Jeri Steele for helping us out of many a dead end. Gratitude is also due to Michael Sprague and Brad Schepp, our editors, and the folks at North Market Street Graphics.

To my family and friends, who patiently waited for me to emerge from the writing frenzy, and especially Marianne, Matthew, and Mark, who were the best support a writing mom and wife ever had, a big thank you.

But most of all I want to thank my mother, Frances Spencer Powell, who urged and encouraged me, babysat and researched for me, and traveled and travailed with me ever since I first got the idea to do a book about online genealogy.

—ELIZABETH P. CROWE

I would like to thank everyone involved in making this project a success. In particular, I would like to thank Margot at Waterside Productions for finding this project, Michael and Libbi for believing I could get it done on schedule, and all the folks at America Online, McGraw-Hill, and Waterside who worked quietly in the background to make it actually happen.

Most important of all, I want to give my deepest thanks to the thousands of people who create, contribute to, and support the genealogy resources on AOL and the Web.

—BILL MANN

Introduction

"Everyman is an omnibus in which his ancestors ride."
—Dr. Oliver Wendell Holmes

Welcome to the America Online edition of *Genealogy Online*. You're about to embark on an adventure that combines a field of study that is thousands of years old (genealogy), with a set of tools that didn't even exist when our parents were born (personal computers, America Online, and the Internet).

A focus of genealogical research is finding the right information. If you live in Topeka you probably can't hop over to Tashkent or Timbuktu to consult birth records on a possible ancestor. But with the amazing amounts of information now available online, you might be able to find that Tashkent birth record without ever leaving your house.

The online world not only gives you access to information but it also gives you access to people. Thanks to technologies like America Online forums, e-mail, newsgroups, mailing lists, and the World Wide Web, you can easily communicate with others who share your interest in genealogy, no matter where in the world they may be.

There are immeasurable amounts of genealogical information, and tens of thousands of genealogy people, online. This book will put you in contact with them. The rest is up to you.

Who Should Read This Book

This book is written for anyone interested in doing genealogical research with the help of a computer. In particular, it is written for America Online members.

This book doesn't attempt to teach you genealogy, but it *can* help even the greenest beginner get started. That's because this book tells you where to find genealogy guidelines for beginners.

So if you're interested in genealogy, have access to a computer (or are willing to buy one), and are a member of AOL, this book is for you.

Background Information for Genealogy Newcomers

While we're not going to attempt to teach genealogy in this book, we do feel it is important to give you a bit of background information on this important field of study.

When you study genealogy, you trace your own place in history. Your results can be shown in charts, trees, circles, quilts, scrapbooks, or even a published book. In the process of researching your family, you are bound to learn about history, law, sociology, and eugenics. Most amateur genealogists find that history means so much more when they see exactly how it affected and shaped their own families.

A major appeal of genealogy is that it provides people with a sense of continuity and of belonging, for the hobby teaches you one thing very quickly: mathematically, we all must be kin somehow. This sense of belonging extends to other genealogists, for it is almost impossible to research any family line by yourself.

It's not as hard to find some information as you might think. Almost any self-respecting public library, no matter how small, has a local history and genealogy section. Some even have entire floors dedicated to those subjects. The Church of Jesus Christ of Latter-Day Saints (the Mormon church) has collected an extensive bank of genealogical data (official registers of births, marriages, and deaths, and related documents), probably the greatest such collection in existence. Church members use these records in order to bring their ancestors posthumously into the church. The federal government has recently started to put much of its data, such as death records, veterans' records, and so on, in machine-readable databases, which could then be accessible via the Internet. This has genealogists everywhere excited.

Of course, once upon a time your genealogy determined your status in society, and even today it may be the deciding factor in inheritance disputes. But usually, pedigree doesn't mean what it previously did for social status. Still, this continues to be a fascinating hobby for thousands of people. The United States alone, for example, has numerous genealogical societies that trace people's descent. Some of these are national, but many more are local or regional, such as the Tennessee Valley Genealogical Society or the New England Historical Society. Others are specific to certain names. Many patriotic organizations, such as the Daughters of the Confederacy, limit membership to descendants of a particular historical group.

How Computers Assist Genealogists

Computers can assist genealogists in many ways. A computer is good for storing huge amounts of data. Computers can also manipulate this data quickly and with 100 percent accuracy. But this isn't the greatest service computers can render to genealogists. Their greatest service is in communications.

As mentioned earlier, getting information is the biggest problem many genealogists face. When connected to networks, computers provide a new way to get information. Once you go online (get connected to AOL or the Internet), you will find vast repositories of genealogical information. Perhaps more important, you will find thousands of other genealogists willing to share information or just help beginners become part of the online genealogical community.

There are many different systems and services that allow you to communicate with others by computer. In this book, you'll learn about the following systems and services: e-mail, America Online, and the Internet.

E-mail Systems

An electronic mail (e-mail) system is a way to transfer messages from you at your computer to someone at another computer. When it arrives at its destination, an e-mail message is stored in the recipient's electronic mailbox to be read at their leisure. In many ways, e-mail messages are the online equivalent of U.S. mail. However, e-mail messages tend to travel much faster than U.S. mail, and can do things that U.S. mail cannot. E-mail messages can carry simple text messages or more complex information like graphics, sound effects, and even video clips. These can take the form of special files attached to the e-mail message. And, using AOL's address book function, a single e-mail message can be easily duplicated and automatically distributed to two, ten, or ten thousand people.

The characteristics of e-mail systems make them ideal tools for genealogists. Because AOL's e-mail system can communicate with the Internet, you can quickly share information with people located virtually anywhere in the world. Since most e-mail systems accept files attached to your messages, you can send and receive information that would be impractical to transfer as text. The ease with which one message can be duplicated and distributed to any number of recipients is quite valuable, too, as you will see in the upcoming discussion of mailing lists.

America Online

America Online (AOL) is the largest online service in the world. Once you connect to AOL, your computer becomes a multimedia window into a marvelous collection of information, services, and people. AOL's mail system is famous for being user-friendly. With it, you can communicate with AOL's 12 million members as well as Internet users. AOL members are reported to send more that 20 million e-mail messages each day! Tens of thousands of genealogy fans are online with America Online, so you'll never be short of people to swap information with, gossip with, or ask for help.

But America Online has far more to offer than just e-mail. AOL members have complete access to the Golden Gate Genealogy Forum, an online gathering place for genealogists and genealogical information. This forum contains files full of information, guidelines for how to get started, and chat areas where you can hold real-time conversations (by typing your messages, not speaking them) with genealogists from around the world. Other forums on AOL also contain valuable genealogical information.

In addition, AOL gives you access to the Internet services such as the World Wide Web, Usenet newsgroups, and mailing lists.

The Internet

The Internet (the Net) is the ultimate computer network. In actuality, the Internet is a network of computer networks, collectively spanning the globe and connecting tens or hundreds of millions of computers and users. The Net is host to a number of information services, each with its own characteristics and rules.

While the variety and immensity of the Internet can make it confusing, it is a treasure trove of genealogy information if you know your way around. Some of the Internet services this book will teach you to use are:

- World Wide Web—the graphically oriented part of the Internet that makes using the Net a point-and-click operation
- Mailing lists—small clubs, newsletters and discussions distributed by e-mail
- Newsgroups—worldwide bulletin boards of discussions and announcements, accessed by the AOL newsreader
- FTP—a system for moving files from one computer to another

How This Book Is Organized

This book is designed to make finding your way to the best genealogical resources on AOL and the Internet quick and easy. After a short discussion of what's needed to get online, you'll progress to America Online, which is designed to make being online easy for anyone. From there, you'll move to the more confusing world of the Internet. After the Net, it's on to other useful but idiosyncratic resources like online library card catalogs and the Tiny Tafel Matching System (a way to query people about your genealogy research needs).

By the time you reach the end of the book, you should be well on your way to becoming an online genealogy expert.

Part 1: The Basics

Before you can do genealogical research online, you need to get online. This part is dedicated to giving you the information you need to do exactly that.

Chapter 1: Getting Started.   Chapter 1 describes the computer hardware and software you need to run America Online 4.0 and walks you through the upgrade process.

Part 2: Genealogy on America Online

There is no better place to start your online genealogy adventures than America Online. AOL is not only rich in genealogical resources, but it is also the largest online service on earth. Where better to meet and share information with others? The chapters in this part guide you to the best genealogy information on America Online.

Chapter 2: The Golden Gate Genealogy Forum. The Genealogy Forum is the center of genealogical activity on America Online. From the Beginners' Center to the Genealogy chat rooms and the Resource Center, this forum is an incredibly rich resource. It also gives you a direct path to the best genealogical resources on the Internet through carefully chosen hyperlinks.

Chapter 3: Other Genealogy Resources on America Online. While the Golden Gate Genealogy Forum is the center of America Online genealogical activity, it isn't the only place an online genealogist will want to visit. This chapter takes you on a guided tour of other useful forums like the Adoption Forum, NetNoir (an area dedicated to all things African-American), and SeniorNet.

Part 3: Genealogy on the Internet

If you thought America Online was big, wait until you get out onto the Internet. Sometimes it seems like every bit of information known to human beings is available on the Net (someday it may be). But the Internet can be as chaotic as it is huge. The chapters in this part will introduce you to several useful Internet services and show you how to use them in your genealogical research.

Chapter 4: Mailing Lists. Mailing lists make it easy to do genealogical research by electronic mail (e-mail). Mailing lists come straight to your America Online mailbox and often are moderated and cozy. Mailing lists may have a few hundred participants, rarely more. This chapter is your guide to genealogical mailing lists, including ROOTS-L, the granddaddy of all genealogy mailing lists.

Chapter 5: Newsgroups. Newsgroups are similar to mailing lists, yet different. Usenet is accessed by the Keyword: USENET. Newsgroups rarely are moderated and often lack the cozy feeling of mailing lists. Newsgroups may have thousands of participants. Having said all that, we have to admit that sometimes a genealogy mailing list has a Usenet newsgroup that mirrors every message word for word. Furthermore you can use the America Online feature called Automated Sessions to download Usenet messages with your e-mail. We'll explain it all to you in this chapter.

America Online gives you access to many valuable genealogy newsgroups, and this chapter shows you what you need to know to put newsgroups to work for you. It also describes some of the genealogy newsgroups you can reach from America Online.

Chapter 6: The World Wide Web. The World Wide Web (the Web) is the multimedia part of the Internet, and this part gets the most attention from the media and general public. With a Web browser, you can take advantage of the fine genealogy sites on the Web and access to many other

Internet services. This chapter will get you up and running on the Web, using America Online's built-in Web browser (Microsoft Internet Explorer). This chapter explores several of the most interesting genealogy Web sites in detail and lists many other sites you can explore on your own.

Chapter 7: AOL NetFind and Other Search Engines.   Search engines and directories help you find resources on the Internet. America Online has AOL NetFind, an Internet search engine that can help you find the genealogical information you need, wherever it may be on the Net. This chapter is a detailed guide to using AOL NetFind to search newsgroups and Web sites. In addition, it covers several other general search engines and directories that are of use to the online genealogist.

Part 4: Other Genealogical Resources

America Online and Internet services like mailing lists or the Web aren't the only online genealogy resources you should know about. The chapters in this part cover two online resources that may be useful to your genealogical research.

Chapter 8: Online Library Card Catalogs.   Many libraries now make their card catalogs available online. This chapter shows you how you can save time and effort in your genealogical research by using online card catalogs.

Chapter 9: The Church of Jesus Christ of Latter-Day Saints.   The Mormons have what are probably the most extensive computerized genealogical databases in the world. Unfortunately, you can't connect to them through America Online or the Internet. You can, however, make use of these computerized resources if you're willing to go to the site. This chapter gives you the basics on getting access to and using the vast genealogical resources held by the Church of Jesus Christ of Latter-Day Saints in their Family History Libraries.

Appendixes

Appendix A: GenServ.   With over 12 million names, the GenServ system is another vast repository of genealogical data that you can reach using the World Wide Web or by sending commands through e-mail and receiving the data by e-mail. This appendix gives you all the information you need, both pro and con, to decide whether you should spend the money to subscribe to GenServ.

Appendix B: The Tiny Tafel Matching System.   The Tiny Tafel Matching System is a way to let other people know what genealogical information you have available and how to contact you. This appendix explains the system and tells you how to use it.

PART 1

The Basics

This part of the book gives you a brief overview of America Online (AOL), then goes on to tell you what you need to know to get upgraded to AOL 4.0 and start researching your roots. The brief description of AOL begins here. The things you need to know to get started are covered in Chapter 1.

AOL is open 24 hours a day and seven days a week. At various out-of-the-way times (early in the morning or late at night) parts of AOL are shut down briefly for maintenance, but basically this system is *always* available for your use.

The basic rates for the service vary, with unlimited use running $21.95 per month at this writing. For your $22 you get complete access to AOL's own content as well as the Internet. On the Internet, you have a Web browser, newsreader, electronic mail, FTP, and telnet.

AOL's Golden Gate Genealogy Forum is among its most popular offerings. This resource alone may be worth the membership fee to budding genealogists. However, as you'll soon learn, there's much more to explore than the Genealogy Forum.

In this book, we're assuming that you'll be using the latest version of the AOL software, version 4.0. If you're using an older version, much of the information will still apply. However, what you see on your screen may differ somewhat from the screens appearing in this book.

CHAPTER 1

Getting Started

As with most things, you can't just jump into online genealogy without some preparation. But the amount and type of preparation you must do depends on where you are now with regard to computers, the Internet, and America Online.

Upgrading to AOL 4.0

To run America Online 4.0, you need a Macintosh computer or a personal computer (PC) that uses the Windows 3.1, Windows 95, Windows NT 4.0, Windows 98, or Windows NT 5.0 operating system. Since America Online gives you complete access to the Internet, once you can connect to AOL you will be able to use Internet resources as well.

The following bulleted lists give the AOL 4.0 system requirements.

System Requirements for Computers Running Windows 95 or Later and Windows NT 4.0 or Later

- 16 megabytes RAM system configuration
- Pentium-class PC
- 45 megabytes available hard disk space
- 640 × 480, 256 colors screen resolution, or better
- 14.4-Kbps modem, or faster

System Requirements for Computers Running Windows 3.1

- 16 megabytes RAM system configuration
- 486-class PC, or better
- 30 megabytes available hard disk space
- 256-color monitor and matching video card
- 640 × 480, 256 colors screen resolution, or better
- 14.4-Kbps modem, or faster

System Requirements for Macintosh Computers

- 12 megabytes RAM system configuration
- System 7.1, or better
- 68040 or PowerPC Macintosh
- 256-color monitor and matching video card
- 640 × 480, 256 colors screen resolution, or better
- 14.4-Kbps modem, or faster

If you need to upgrade any system components, be sure to visit AOL's Hardware Shop at Keyword: *Hardware Center*. Users with Windows 95 machines that don't meet the AOL 4.0 for Windows 95 requirements can use the 16-bit version (the version that is normally used with Windows 3.1).

What You Should Do Next

Now that you know if your computer meets the system requirements, what you should do next varies. The following list will direct you to the right section of the chapter.

- If your computer doesn't meet the AOL 4.0 system requirements, skip down to the section entitled "What to Do if Your System Doesn't Measure Up."
- If your computer meets the AOL 4.0 system requirements and you are satisfied with what you have, you can skip down to the section called "Installing America Online 4.0 on a Windows 95 PC."
- If your computer meets the system requirements, but you would like to get the most out of America Online and the Internet, consider upgrading your modem to one of the high-speed models now available. Skip to the section entitled "About Conventional Modems" for some background information.
- If you plan to connect to America Online using an ISDN terminal adapter, a cable modem, or a direct connection, skip reading the instructions for installing America Online on a Windows 95 PC, then skip down to "Other Ways to Connect to America Online" for specific information on making the connection.

What to Do if Your System Doesn't Measure Up

If you're running Windows 95 or Windows 98, but your system doesn't measure up, you have several options. If your machine meets the Windows 3.1 requirements, you can run the AOL 4.0 for Windows 3.1 software.

If you don't have enough space on your hard drive to meet the system requirements, see if there are old files or programs you can remove from the system. By deleting things you don't use (or backing them up to disk or tape) you may be able to free enough space to meet the system requirements. Another option is to add a second hard drive to increase the storage capacity of your computer.

If you can't bring your computer up to the system requirements, you may still be able to run America Online version 4.0, but you will experience a much slower response time. If this is the case, you should seriously consider upgrading your computer. America Online doesn't have very stringent system requirements. If your computer has trouble meeting them, it is likely holding you back in other areas, too. Computers with more than enough power for America Online are available for around $1000. A trip to your local computer superstore may be in order.

You can likely upgrade your computer to meet the AOL 4.0 system requirements. To do so, determine which bits of your system don't measure up, then start replacing them. The place to shop for upgrade components is the AOL Store (Keyword: *AOL Store*). As you can see in Fig. 1-1, the AOL Store has several sections of interest to people who are upgrading their machines. The Hardware and Modems sections will have the parts you need to bring your system up to snuff. For advice, check the Upgrade Tips and Tech Support areas in the Hardware area, and the Modem Help area under Modems.

Installing America Online on a Windows 95 PC

To connect to and use America Online, you need the America Online software. This software is free—AOL makes its money on the monthly fees you pay to use the service. It's sort of like the story about the razor and the blades. Companies will happily give away their razors for free, because they make their money on the blades you must keep buying. But the America Online software is probably easier to find than a free razor.

Figure 1-1

The AOL Store stocks the parts you need to get your computer ready for AOL 4.0.

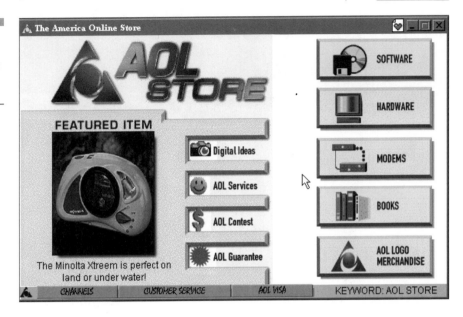

As with most commercial online services, the only way you can get access to the contents of the AOL service is through the proprietary America Online software. This software makes America Online a colorful, easy-to-use place in cyberspace.

As a computer user, you've probably received one or more AOL disks or CD-ROMs in the mail within the past several months. You can use one of them to start your account. Or, if you don't have an AOL disk or CD-ROM, you can usually find the software attached to a magazine in some bookstore. You can also call AOL at (800) 827-6364 and request the software on CD-ROM.

Installing the AOL Software

Insert the floppy disk or CD-ROM that contains the AOL software and follow the directions on the package to start installing the software. Your computer screen will look like Fig. 1-2. Click **Install** to start the process.

The installation process is almost totally automated. First the AOL software will decompress its files and copy them to your hard drive. While this is happening, you'll see a bar graph that shows you what percentage of the files have been manipulated so far (Fig. 1-3).

From here, all you really need to do is follow the on-screen instructions and answer a few questions, like the one shown in Fig. 1-4. The America Online software does all the work for you.

Figure 1-2
Choose the correct
option for your
system: new user,
upgrading, or adding.

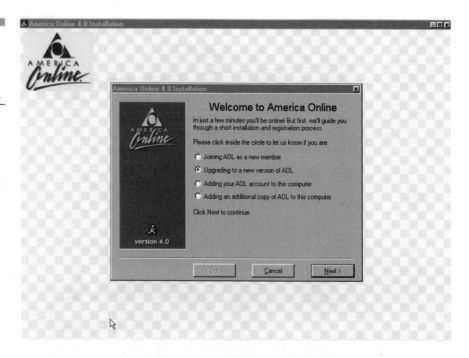

Eventually you'll see a message box like the one in Fig. 1-5. This tells you that the first part of the installation is complete. You have the software installed and ready to go, but you don't yet have an active account on America Online. Follow the directions in the message box to go online and activate your account.

NOTE *If you are using something other than a standard modem to connect to AOL, you should skip down to the appropriate section of this chapter to see what you must do to make the AOL connection.*

When you start the AOL software for the first time, you'll find that the instructions and procedures are very thorough, as Fig. 1-6 illustrates. With millions of members, the AOL staff has had a *lot* of experience getting people connected to the service for the first time. If you just stick with the written and on-screen instructions, you should have no trouble getting AOL installed and running.

Soon you'll be looking at the Sign On screen (Fig. 1-7). Selecting a screen name for the first time is one of the few potentially confusing steps in the

Figure 1-3
The AOL software always keeps you informed on the progress of the installation.

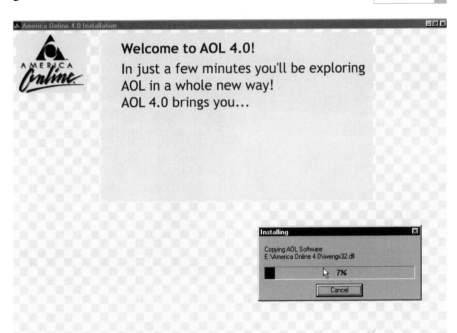

Figure 1-4
The installation program uses simple dialog boxes like this one to ask you the few questions it needs you to answer.

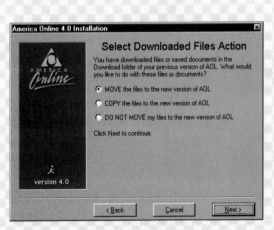

Figure 1-5

When you see a message box like this one, you'll know you have the AOL software installed. The next step is setting up your account.

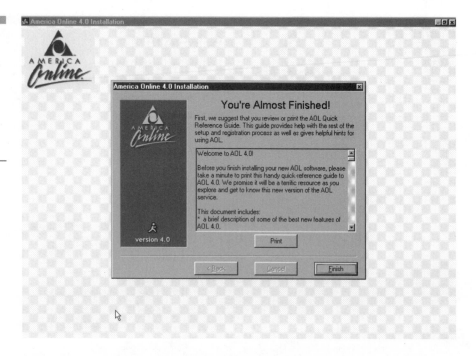

Figure 1-6

Thorough instructions that cover all eventualities make it easy to set up your America Online account.

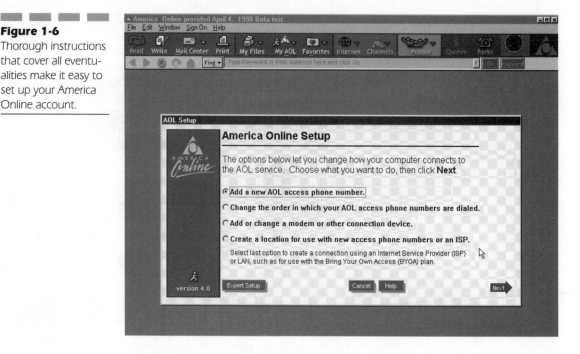

entire installation process. You can just click **SIGN ON** and in most cases everything will go smoothly from there. If you have a problem, click **Help**.

NOTE   *Be sure to have your credit card or checking account information handy when you connect to the service. You'll need to enter that information, even if you are on a 50-free-hour membership. That way, the folks at America Online have the information to bill you if you exceed your set number of free hours.*

As you follow the registration instructions, you'll come to a point where you can enter your screen name. Your screen name is the name that people will know you by when you are connected to AOL. Choose this carefully, for you cannot change it without closing the old account and starting a new one. However, you may have up to five screen names assigned to the main account, so each family member can have a mailbox, a set of favorites, and a place to file messages and downloads.

You'll also need to choose a password. Keep this secret—*never* give it to anyone on AOL, even if they claim to be one of the staff. No one from AOL will *ever* ask you for your password online.

Figure 1-7
When you see this window you are almost ready to go online.

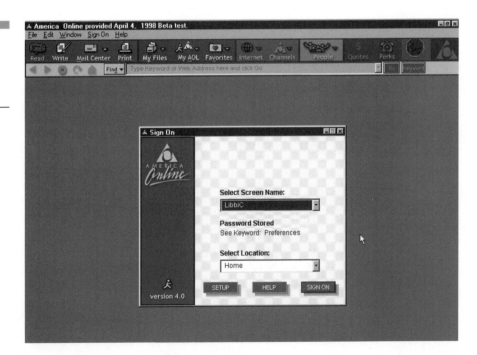

Your screen name can be a variation of your real name, but with over 12 million AOL members, it's hard to find a name that hasn't been used yet. More likely, your choice of name will be taken, and AOL will suggest one based on your name but with a bunch of numbers attached to it. If your America Online screen name is jsmith, then your e-mail address when communicating with AOL members is jsmith. When communicating with other people on the Internet, your e-mail address is your_screen_name@aol.com.

NOTE   You'll learn a lot more about e-mail addresses, and e-mail in general, in Chapter 4. When you complete the registration process, you can go online to America Online.

Getting Around in America Online

America Online provides you with several ways to move around the service. One way is just to click on the names or icons of places you want to visit. Say you've connected to AOL and are looking at the AOL screen (Fig. 1-8), one of the options you can choose is AOL Today.

One of the best places to start learning about America Online is the AOL Quickstart Guide. The first time you sign on you'll see a window offering you a tour, and you can click on it to get to the Quickstart Guide.

NOTE   You can tell when you are pointing at something you can click on, because your mouse pointer changes from an arrow to a pointing hand.

When you click on the AOL Quickstart Guide icon, the mouse pointer turns into an hourglass for a few seconds; then a new window appears on the screen. This one is titled QuickStart: a Guide for New Members. When you visit this area of AOL, make sure to click on the topics listed on the left side of the window. These will give you a thorough introduction to using America Online.

One thing to notice about the QuickStart: a Guide for New Members window is the text in the bottom right corner. It says Keyword: *QuickStart,* and refers to another way to get around America Online. Keywords are

Figure 1-8
Whenever you
connect to America
Online, you'll start
with a version of
this screen.

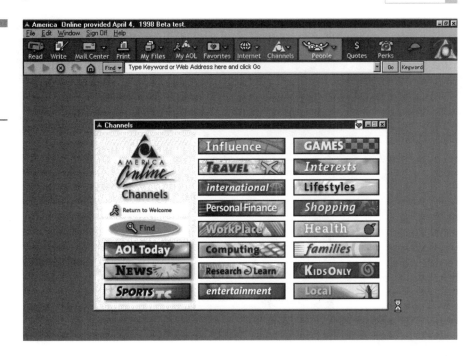

shortcuts to specific areas of America Online. If you know the keyword
for the area you want to go to, you can go there directly, instead of clicking your way through multiple screens of information.

Look for the address box in the AOL 4.0 screen. It says: "Type Keyword
or Web Address here and click Go." Another way to enter a keyword is to
click the button on the toolbar that says **KEYWORD** or press **CTRL-K**
(the Control or CTRL key and the K key simultaneously). This opens the
Keyword window (Fig. 1-9), where you can type in the keyword you want.
Click Go to go to the window or area identified by the keyword you
entered. The Quickstart Guide contains a list of general keywords that
you should know.

NOTE   *When you enter a keyword, exact spelling is necessary, but capitalization is unimportant. In other words, genealogy and Genealogy are the same keyword, but QuickStart and QuickStrt are not.*

You can also use this window to search AOL for topics of interest. To
do this, click the FIND button to the left of the address box. You will have

Figure 1-9
Use keywords in the
address box or by
using the KEYWORD
button or Control-K.
Enter the keyword
and click on GO.

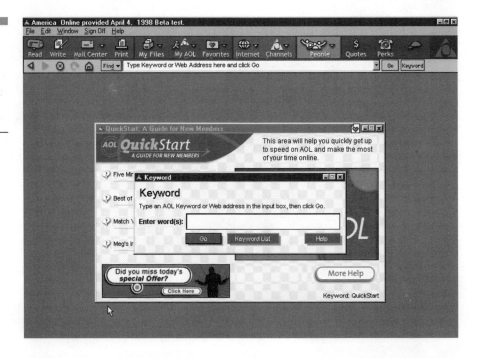

a choice of looking on America Online only, or over the entire Web using
AOL NetFind.

NOTE   *As you move around AOL, new windows open, but the old ones don't
close. You'll want to keep the clutter down by closing some old windows when
you no longer need them.*

Keyword: *Genealogy*

As an online genealogist, one keyword you'll use a lot is Keyword: *Genealogy.* Enter that keyword to get to the America Online Golden Gate
Genealogy Forum. You can also set things up so that AOL takes you right
to the Golden Gate Genealogy Forum when you're online. Here's how:
Start the America Online software, but don't sign on to the service yet.
Click the **Favorites** button in the toolbar, then click **My Shortcuts** and
then **Edit Shortcuts**. You'll see the window in Fig. 1-10. This is the **Shortcut Keys** menu.

If you enter the words Golden Gate Genealogy Forum in an open spot of the left-hand column (the Key column) and the word Genealogy (Roots also works) in the corresponding slot in the Keyword column, you can go directly to the forum. In Fig. 1-10, this has been done with row 1. Be sure to click the **Save Changes** button. Now, whenever we're on AOL, typing **CTRL**+1 (the Control or CTRL key and the 1 key simultaneously) means that we can go directly to the Golden Gate Genealogy Forum.

NOTE   *These shortcuts only work when you are signed on to America Online. They won't start the service for you.*

You now have enough information to start your online genealogy research at America Online. You can stop reading right here, and skip to Chap. 2, where you'll get an in-depth tour of the Golden Gate Genealogy Forum. Or, you can continue reading here to learn more about modems, alternatives to modems, and America Online version 4.0 software. It's up to you.

Figure 1-10
You can edit the
Shortcut Keys menu
to take you quickly to
the Golden Gate
Genealogy Forum.

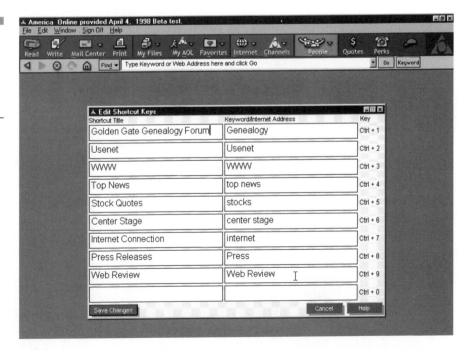

About Conventional Modems

If you don't have a modem, or your modem doesn't meet the recommended speed, 28.8 Kbps (28,800 bits per second), you need a new modem. For that matter, even if your modem does measure up to the minimum standards, you may still want to consider buying a new modem. While a modem that runs at 28.8 Kbps (sometimes known as a 28.8 or twenty-eight eight modem) is fast enough to work with America Online, you'll be a lot happier with a faster modem. Conventional modems can now run almost twice the speed of a 28.8 modem.

To understand what is going on with modems well enough to make an informed decision about buying a new one, you'll need to follow us through a little bit of techno-geek terminology. We promise not to make it too painful.

Conventional modems are the slowest way to connect to AOL, but they're also the most common, least expensive, and easiest to get set up. A conventional modem connects to AOL using the plain old telephone system (POTS). Today, the fastest conventional modems are rated at 56 Kbps, although in practice they seldom attain that speed.

Modems are usually described by the speed at which they can send or receive data. As we've already explained, the minimum speed modem you want to use with America Online is a 28.8-Kbps modem. But you really want to connect with a faster modem than that. 33.6-Kbps modems are really the slowest ones generally available today.

High-Speed Modems and AOLnet

America Online has its own high-speed communication network that supports 28.8 Kbps and faster modems. Known as AOLnet, this network is available across much of the United States. To find out more about AOLnet, high-speed modem access, 800-number access, and even to shop for a new modem, log on to AOL and go to Keyword: *Access* (Fig. 1-11).

NOTE *While AOLnet is designed to allow high-speed modems to run at their best speed, there are no guarantees. Here is what America Online has to say on the subject: "Connection speeds may vary, much as 56-Kbps connections do. These numbers support speeds up to 56 Kbps, but local telephone equipment and telephone wiring in the home also impact the rate of the connection. There is no*

guarantee you will connect to the numbers at higher speeds than your regular access numbers."

While you're at the Access window, you may want to click on the Modem Shop. Here you can buy AOL-tested modems by many different manufacturers that work well with the AOL service.

Other Ways to Connect to America Online

The speed of your connection to America Online makes a big difference in your enjoyment of AOL or the Internet. With a slow connection, it takes much longer for information to appear on your computer screen. With a fast connection, you spend much less time waiting for information to appear on the screen and a lot more time actually doing productive genealogical research.

Alternatives to modems can give you a connection that's much faster than the fastest modem can possibly go. That's because there are inherent limits in how fast information can travel over phone lines. The modems you can buy today are already faster than many people believed possible only a few years ago, and there is little chance that conventional modems will exceed the 56-Kbps speeds they're reaching now. So if you want a really fast connection to America Online or the Internet, you need to find an alternative to the conventional modem.

You are only likely to encounter three alternatives to the conventional modem in the next few years. These are cable modems (which aren't modems at all, despite their names), ISDN (Integrated Services Digital Network) terminal adapters, and direct connections to the Internet (and from there to America Online) across a corporate LAN (local area network). You can read more about these, and AOL's latest capabilities in these areas, at Keyword: *HIGHSPEED*. The following sections provide a layman's guide to these three alternatives.

Cable Modems

Cable modems are really just a way to connect to a high-speed digital information network run by a cable television company. The cable com-

Figure 1-11
Get the answers to
your AOL access
questions by visiting
the Accessing America
Online area.

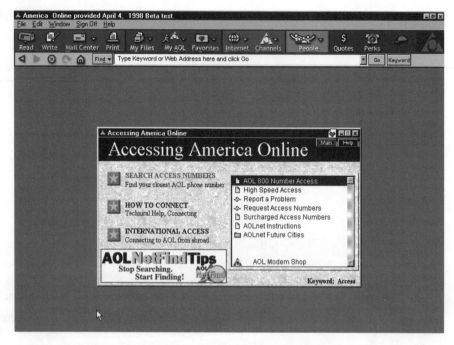

pany serves as an Internet Service Provider (ISP). From the Internet, you
can connect to the AOL network. You still need an America Online
account, so using a cable modem is definitely more expensive than connecting to AOL directly by modem, but the extra money brings you
speed.

Cable modems are far faster than either conventional modems or
ISDN, although they are still relatively rare. One of the authors (Bill) has
a cable modem connection to AOL through the Internet. This connection allows him to receive data from the Net (and AOL) at 1.5 Mbps (about
1.5 million bits per second) and to send information back the other way
at 300 Kbps. The price of cable modem service varies wildly across the
country, but you can get it in some areas for less than $40 per month.
However, cable modem service is generally limited to major metropoli-
tan areas.

Once you have a cable modem connected to your computer and running properly, it's easy to use it to connect to AOL. The instructions provided by America Online worked perfectly for Bill and are reproduced
here.

Making a Cable Modem Connection

America Online's software is completely compatible with any cable modem system. To set your communications settings to receive a signal over a cable line, simply set up your AOL software to connect using TCP/IP over the Internet from your cable modem. Follow the instructions given in the numbered list.

NOTE   *TCP/IP stands for Transmission Control Protocol/Internet Protocol. It's the communications protocol used by computers when they transfer data on the Internet. If you can establish a TCP/IP connection to America Online, you can bypass your modem and use higher speed connection methods like cable modems and ISDN terminal adapters. America Online doesn't charge extra for connecting with TCP/IP.*

1. Connect to your Cable Modem Service Provider (If you need help with this part call your cable company.).
2. Leave that software connected and launch America Online.
3. On the Sign On screen, click the **Setup** button.
4. Click the **Create Location** button.
5. Select **TCP/IP** from the Network drop-down box.
6. Click **Save**.
7. Click **OK** to return to the Sign On screen.
8. Click **Sign On** and you will connect to America Online over the connection of your cable modem.

It really is that simple. Once you try connecting to AOL by cable modem, you'll never want to go back to a conventional modem again.

ISDN Terminal Adapters

ISDN terminal adapters are faster than conventional modems, but slower than cable modems. They can send and receive data at 128 Kbps. They tend to be difficult to get set up and expensive to use. To use an ISDN terminal adapter, you need to get a special digital signal line run to your house from an Internet service provider. The ISP connects your computer to the Internet, and from there you connect to America Online.

As with cable modems, this means you'll need to pay the ISP that provides your ISDN connection, as well as paying America Online for your membership on AOL. You'll also likely have to pay high monthly and per-minute charges to actually own and use an ISDN terminal adapter.

Connecting with ISDN

Assuming you have an ISDN connection to the Internet, it's easy to connect to America Online. You can find out about America Online's current ISDN capabilities at Keyword: *ISDN.* Follow these instructions, which are virtually identical to those for a cable modem:

1. Connect to your Internet service provider (If you need help with this part call your ISP.).
2. Leave that software connected and launch America Online.
3. On the Sign On screen, click the **Setup** button.
4. Click the **Create Location** button.
5. Select **TCP/IP** from the Network drop-down box.
6. Click **Save**.
7. Click **OK** to return to the Sign On screen.
8. Click **Sign On** and you will connect to America Online over the connection of your cable modem.

Direct Connections

If you are using AOL at work, and your company has a direct connection to the Internet through the corporate LAN, you can use that to connect to America Online. As with cable modems and ISDN terminal adapters, you connect to the Net, and use the Net to connect to America Online. For this to work, your company network must support TCP/IP as one of its protocols.

▬ ▬ ▬ ▬ ▬ ▬ ▬ ▬ ▬ ▬ ▬ ▬ ▬ ▬ ▬ ▬ ▬

NOTE   If you have trouble making the connection to AOL, or don't know if the network supports TCP/IP, contact your network administrator. Follow these steps for direct connection:

1. Connect to your corporate network (if you don't have a full-time connection).

2. Leave that software connected and launch America Online.

3. On the Sign On screen, click the **Setup** button.

4. Click the **Create Location** button.

5. Select **TCP/IP** from the Network drop-down box.

6. Click **Save**.

7. Click **OK** to return to the Sign On screen.

8. Click **Sign On** and you will connect to America Online over the connection of your cable modem.

2

Genealogy on America Online

There is no better place to start your online genealogy adventures than America Online (AOL). This easy-to-use service is not only rich in genealogical resources, but it's also the largest online service in existence. One recent study stated that about 60 percent of all the online time that people spend when at home is time spent connected to AOL. What better place could there be to meet and share information with other people who are into genealogy? The chapters in this section are your introduction to the genealogy resources on America Online.

CHAPTER 2

The Golden Gate Genealogy Forum

The Genealogy Forum (Keyword: *ROOTS* or *GENEALOGY*) is the center of genealogical activity on America Online. From the Beginners' Center to the Genealogy chat rooms and the Resource Center, this forum is an incredibly rich resource. The Forum's tens of thousands of members make it the largest genealogical society in the world, online or off. Figure 2-1 shows the Golden Gate Genealogy Forum main window.

NOTE   *As of March 20, 1998, the Genealogy Forum became the Golden Gate Genealogy Forum. The Golden Gate Genealogy Forum on America Online is a production of Golden Gate Services, Inc. of Franklin, Massachusetts. The president of Golden Gate Services is none other than George Ferguson, the forum leader (screen name: GFL George). We think it is safe to say that the forum remains in good hands, and exciting changes in layout and features are ahead. For convenience, we'll just call the forum the Genealogy Forum throughout the rest of the chapter.*

Don't forget to add the Genealogy Forum to your list of Favorite Places. To do this, just click the heart on the top right side of the forum main window.

Figure 2-1
The Golden Gate Genealogy Forum. Details will change from time to time, but the basic choices will remain the same.

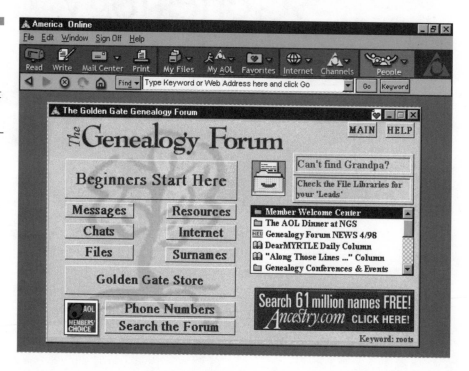

Member Welcome Center

On your first visit to the Genealogy Forum, plan to spend some time in the Member Welcome Center (Fig. 2-2). You get there by double clicking the folder labeled Member Welcome Center in the Genealogy Forum Main Menu.

In the center, you'll be able to read about the people who keep the Genealogy Forum running, see how the forum is managed, and find out about upcoming genealogy conferences and events. Most important, you'll be able to read the Genealogy Forum Frequently Asked Question (FAQ) files.

FAQ files are important things to look for in any AOL forum, as well as in electronic mailing lists, newsgroups, and at Web sites. The FAQ files are collections of the most commonly asked questions pertaining to the forum, list, newsgroup, or site. Read these files before you start asking questions or posting messages. Online areas like the Genealogy Forum are similar to real-world communities in that they have their own rules of behavior. The FAQ files will give you a basic understanding of the forum from the start.

Figure 2-2
You'll be spending a lot of time in the Genealogy Forum, so visit the Member Welcome Center for background information on the Forum and its staff.

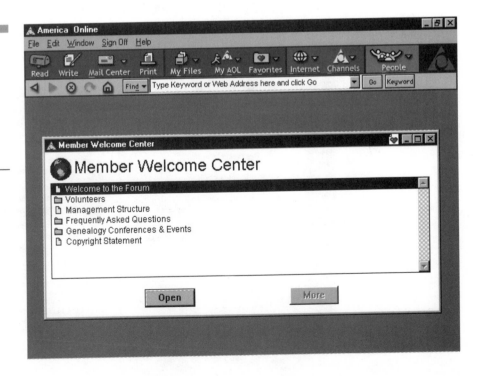

Once you finish with the Member Welcome Center, you have two paths you can follow. One is to head to the Beginners' Center, which is designed for people who are new to genealogy. Or, if you are already a genealogist, you can skip the Beginners' Center and begin with the Quick Start Guide, which tells you how to start researching your roots with the Genealogy Forum.

Beginners' Center

To reach the Beginners' Center you click the big Beginners Start Here button on the Genealogy Forum main window. This takes you to the Genealogy Quick Start window. At the bottom of the window is the **Beginners' Center** button. Click this button and you'll see a window similar to the one in Fig. 2-3. As you can see in the figure, the Beginners' Center has lots of useful tools and information. Each major section of the center is described in the sections that follow.

Figure 2-3

The Beginners' Center is a perfect starting place for people who are new to the world of genealogy.

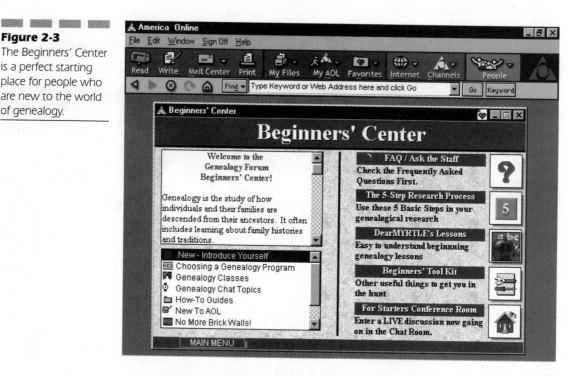

FAQ/Ask the Staff

Click the **FAQ/Ask the Staff** button to see a list of frequently asked questions (Fig. 2-4). This list is identical to the one you'll find in the Member Welcome Center, except for the last item in the list. The last item is **ASK THE STAFF.** Click it and you'll get to send e-mail directly to one of the Genealogy Forum staff members.

The 5-Step Research Process

The 5-step research process is a systematic approach to doing any genealogical research. This is an excellent tutorial on how to get started in genealogy. According to the process, Family History Research is asking yourself the same questions, in order, in cycles.

1. What do I already know?

2. What specific question needs to be answered?

3. What records might answer my question?

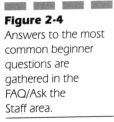

Figure 2-4
Answers to the most common beginner questions are gathered in the FAQ/Ask the Staff area.

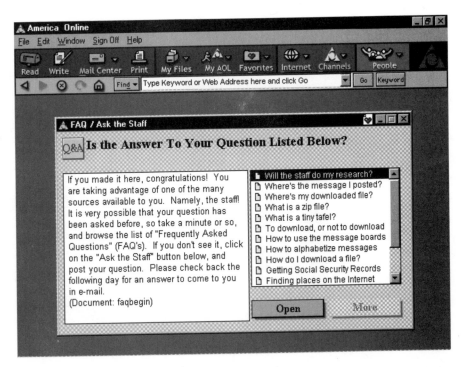

4. What do the records actually tell me?

5. What conclusions can I reach now?

Click the **5-Step Research Process** button to open the window (Fig. 2-5) and start applying the process to your research today.

DearMYRTLE's Beginner Lessons

Begun in January 1997, DearMYRTLE's Beginning Genealogy Lessons (Fig. 2-6) are weekly text files on aspects of genealogical research for the beginner. They are well worth saving for future reference.

Beginners' Tool Kit

The Beginners' Tool Kit (Fig. 2-7) is a grab bag of information files, from how to get addresses to what different forms you can use to display your research.

Figure 2-5
The 5-Step Research Process is a system for making your genealogical research fast and efficient.

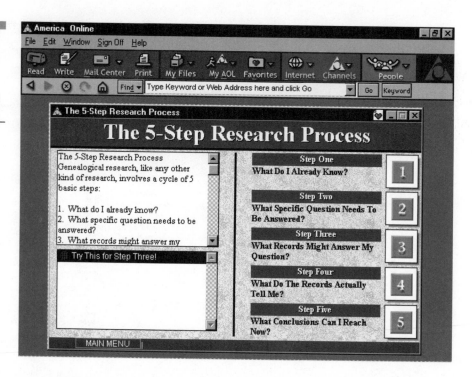

Figure 2-6

This area has dozens of genealogy lessons taken from Myrtle's weekly column.

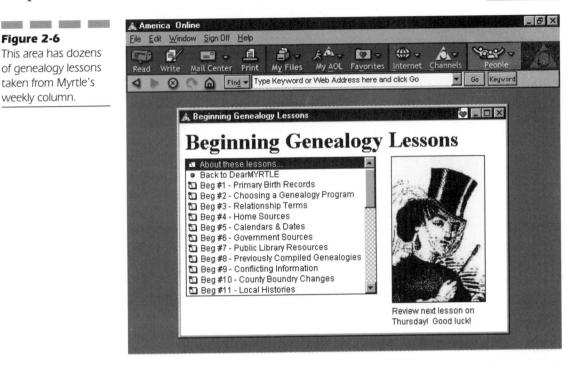

Figure 2-7

The Beginners' Tool Kit contains links to all sorts of resources and information, both on AOL and off.

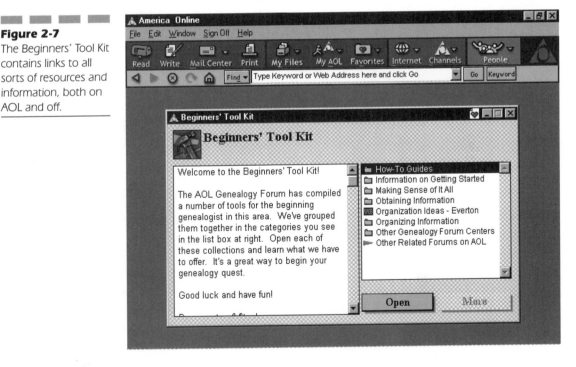

There are all sorts of gems in the toolkit. Do you want to learn about colonial diseases and cures? Can't figure out a genealogical abbreviation? If so, this is the part of the Genealogy Forum for you. Here you'll find guides on getting started in genealogy, organizing your data as you get more experienced, tips on how to get information (who to write, how to ask), and links to related services on America Online.

For Starters Conference Room

If you want to talk to other beginners exploring genealogy on AOL, click the button for the **For Starters Conference Room**. Here you'll find beginners asking questions and generally chatting back and forth on genealogy.

Other Resources

Still more genealogy resources for beginners are found in the menu on the bottom left side of the Beginners' Center window. There is an assortment of information here, including such valuable items as a suggested reading list, genealogy supply companies, and a guide to choosing a Genealogy program (Fig. 2-8).

Quick Start Guide

If you're already a practicing genealogist, you can skip the Beginners' Center, and start with the Genealogy Quick Start Guide. The guide tells you how to put the resources of the Genealogy Forum to work for you immediately. To reach it, you click **Beginners Start Here** on the Genealogy Forum main window.

The Quick Start Guide has four sections, each describing specific resources within the forum and telling you how to use them. The four sections are:

1. *Search by topic.*   The fastest way to search in the Genealogy Forum. Most people begin by typing in one surname to see what pops up. You can also put in a geographical term (Ohio, France) and see what files and articles there might be.

2. *Surname message boards.*   Use these to look up a surname directly.

Figure 2-8
Looking for a geneal-
ogy computer pro-
gram? Visit the GSP
area for information
and advice.

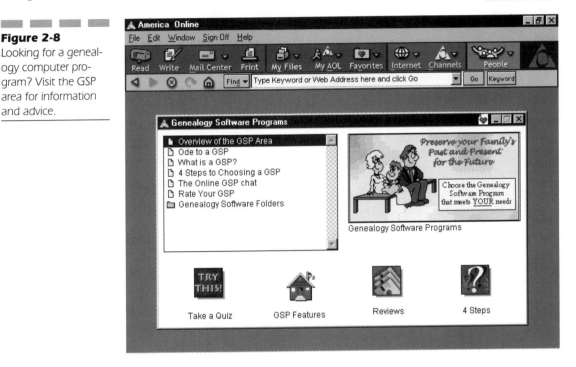

3. *Files library center.*   Look in this area to see if other forum members
   have already uploaded useful material like GEDCOM files that are
   helpful to your research.

4. *Special centers provide additional resources.*   This is a quick introduction
   to some of the other useful resources in the Genealogy Forum, some
   of which we describe below such as the genealogy column
   DearMYRTLE.

Message Boards

The message boards in the Genealogy Forum are the place to post messages when you need information you can't find elsewhere in the forum.
The boards operate on a volunteer basis; you're invited to post any questions you might have and are encouraged to post a reply to anybody else's
question that you have information about. Also, don't forget to post the
family names you're looking for in the message board under the surname
category.

To reach the message boards, click the large **Messages** button in the Genealogy Forum main window. Using the Message Board Center (Fig. 2-9), you can post messages in any of five major subject areas.

- *Surnames.* Post messages asking about specific family names you are researching.

- *The United States.* Post messages about research within specific states or regions of the United States.

- *Countries of the world.* Post messages about research in countries other than the United States.

- *Ethnic and special groups.* Post messages about your research into ethnic or other special groups.

- *Computer and general.* Post messages about topics that don't fit into the other message boards.

Before you start exploring the message boards, it's a good idea to read the messages that appear in the menu on the lower left side of the Message Board Center main window. They explain how the center and the message boards work. In particular, pay attention to the Set Personal Preferences First and How to Read & Compose Offline messages. They can

Figure 2-9
The Message Board Center is the place to read and post messages about a wide range of genealogy topics.

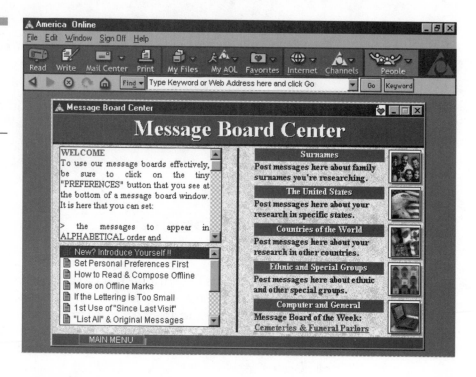

make the Message Board Center much easier to use. Once you've read these messages, you should set your preferences, then start exploring the message boards.

Within each of these message board topic areas, you may find dozens of specific boards. For example, within Surnames there are areas for surnames that begin with each letter of the alphabet. Within those areas are boards for surnames that begin with specific combinations of letters. These finally lead to the actual message boards.

Searching for the surname Mann, we began with the Surnames topic. Under Surnames, we selected the **M Surnames** folder, then the MAN–MBZ Message Board. You'll know when you've reached an actual message board because the icon for it is a green piece of paper with a pushpin through it.

Continuing this example, the MAN–MBZ Message Board (Fig. 2-10) is an example of a specific message board. The large list in the window lists the Subject of each posted message, and the number of postings to each subject. When someone replies to a message that has been posted, it creates a message thread, sort of a conversation on that particular subject. The Postings column tells how many messages are in the thread.

Figure 2-10
Each message board has a set of controls that make it easy to use and customize.

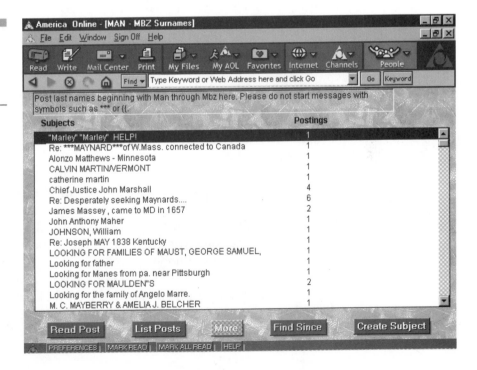

Each board also has a set of controls that make it easy to use and customize. Here is a rundown of the controls and what they do.

- *Read Post.*   This control displays the contents of the message (or message thread) that is selected in the message list.

- *List Posts.*   This control displays a list of relevant information about the message (or message thread) that is selected in the message list.

- *More.*   If you selected More in your preferences, and more messages are available than the message list holds, you can click this button to load more messages into the message list.

- *Find Since.*   Click this if you want to do a search of the message list.

- *Create Subject.*   Click this to create a new subject in the message board.

- *Preferences.*   This button allows you to control how messages appear in the message list.

- *Mark Read.*   Click this to mark the selected messages and threads in this list as read. The list will then treat them according to your preferences, as if you actually read them.

- *Mark All Read.*   Click this to mark all the messages and threads in this list as read. The list will then treat them according to your preferences, as if you actually read all of them.

Reading online isn't bad, but Libbi (one of the authors) finds it much more efficient to read offline, using Automatic AOL and the File Cabinet's Search function. You can only do this with message boards that have been converted to Usenet format (not all of them have been converted). But for those that have, this can be a real time saver.

Here's how to go about it.

Let's say the topic of interest is messages about Powells. First, click on **Message Board Center**. In the top left scroll-down box, move down until you see the link **All Genealogy Forum Message Boards**; click on this link.

When the All Genealogy Forum Message Boards window appears, click on the topic Genealogy Message Boards. (*Tip:* Remember that you can use that heart to put this window in your Favorites!) For this example, you would click **TOP SURNAMES IN THE US**. When you have that window, keep clicking **MORE** until you get to the POWELL message board, highlight it and click the button **Read Offline**. You'll get a message that the board has been added, and to view your list, go to the keyword *My Boards.*

(*Tip:* Remember you can add Keyword My Boards to your shortcuts list!) At the keyword My Boards you can delete message boards from your list, set the maximum number to be downloaded, toggle the read offline setting, and set other preferences for each board on your list.

When you run an Automatic AOL session now, the new messages are retrieved with your e-mail and placed in the Personal Filing Cabinet. Once a session is done, click on **My Files**, and then **Personal Filing Cabinet**. Your message board will be a folder under Newsgroups. To read all the messages, just as you would e-mail or newsgroups, simply open the folder and click on each message. However, you don't really have to look at every one.

To save time, you can use the **Find** button in the Personal Filing Cabinet and look for messages that interest you. Say I want to know about Powells in South Carolina. Now, the **Find** button gives you a choice of searching all folders or only open folders, and either full text or only the subject lines. To make the search faster, open the Powell folder, closing all others, and choose Open Folders. Then choose Full Text or Titles Only, whichever you feel is most likely to get a match. Then enter the term "South Carolina" in the text box and click **Find Next**. If no messages match the search, you can delete all that day's messages, compact the Filing Cabinet, and try another day.

Genealogy Chat Center

The Chat Center (Fig. 2-11) is where you go to hold online, real-time conversations with other genealogists. To get to the Chat Center, click the **Chats** button on the forum's main window. There are chat rooms for many different topics: Beginning Genealogy Chat, Southern Chat, and War Between the States Chat being three examples. Some chats are continuous, some are active at specific times; schedules and lineups appear in the list on the left of the Chat Center main window.

As with the Message Board Center, the first order of business is to read the messages in the menu on the lower left of the Chat Center window. Pay particular attention to the Lineup lists. Since chat is a real-time activity, many sessions are scheduled in advance. If you just want to drop in, one of the five main chat rooms usually has someone in it.

Figure 2-12 shows a chat room. We selected an empty room to avoid reproducing anyone's chat without their permission.

Figure 2-11
Go to the Chat Center for real-time, live chat sessions with other genealogists from around the world.

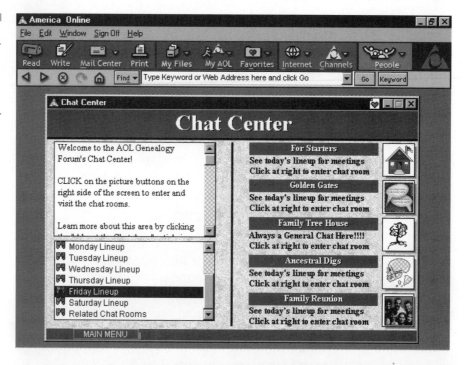

Figure 2-12
A chat session window.

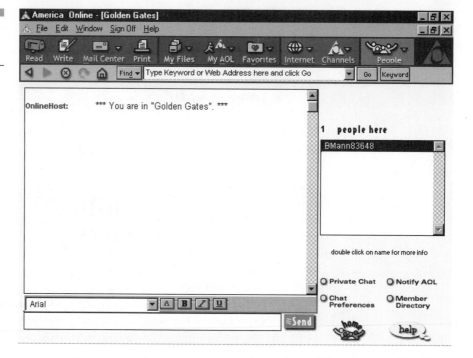

The large window on the left is where the chat messages appear. As new ones arrive, they all shift up the screen, so the newest messages are at the bottom.

Below the chat window is a box where you enter the text of the message you want to send. Click **Send** to transmit the message to the other participants in the chat room.

To the right of the chat window is a list of the people present in the chat room. Right now Bill is the only one there, but the chat rooms can hold dozens of people. To find out more about someone in the chat room, double click their screen name in this list.

Other controls in the chat window include the following.

- *Private Chat.*   This allows you to invite someone in the chat room to chat with you privately.
- *Chat Preferences.*   Click this to set the five chat options available.
- *Notify AOL.*   If someone is misbehaving in the chat, you can click this to report the infraction to AOL.
- *Member Directory.*   This lets you request the profile of a person, whether they are present in the chat room or not.

File Libraries Center

The File Libraries Center (Fig. 2-13) is a central location for all sorts of computer files of interest to genealogists. Split among five sections, each containing multiple libraries, the center has thousands of files you can download.

You'll find files here ranging from trial versions of popular genealogy software to GEDCOMs and other genealogy information from members. You can use the new Library Sort feature to make it easier to find specific files in the libraries, or you can click **Search the Forum** on the main Genealogy Forum window to use the Search Genealogy Forum feature.

Resource Center

The Resource Center is chock full of information to save you lots of trial and error. This area has articles, helps, and tips in the subject of Regions of the World, Ethnic Resources, Vital and other records, and additional

Figure 2-13
Go to the File Libraries
Center to find virtually
any genealogy-related
file you can think of.

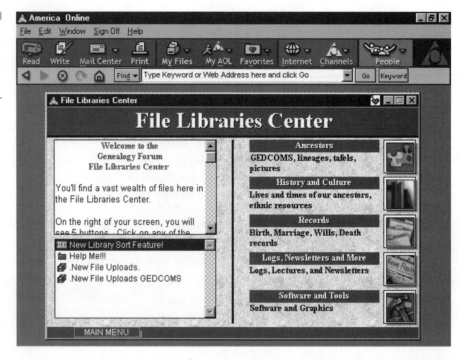

resources. Here you'll find guides and tips to making your research more productive.

To visit the Resource Center you click **Resources** on the main Genealogy Forum window.

Internet Center

The Internet Center in the Genealogy Forum is where you'll find Web sites, FTP and Gopher sites, newsgroups, and mailing lists that specifically have to do with genealogy. This can save you a lot of time as compared to randomly searching the Internet for specific genealogy items. However, if you want to go farther afield, be sure to check out Net Help—the Answer Man, where tips, tricks, and FAQ's about the Internet in general, and AOL's connection in particular, are stored. You can subscribe to newsgroups here, or at the Keyword: *Usenet.* Click on **Expert Add** and type in the soc.genealogy newsgroups you want.

NOTE   *Part 3 of this book covers using the Internet for genealogical research.*

Here's a newsgroups tip: In your Automatic AOL Settings window, check the box "Retrieve unread NewsGroup messages" and the box "Send outgoing NewsGroup messages." Then, when online, go to Keyword: *USENET.* Click on the **Read offline** button. Your subscribed newsgroups will be listed on the left. Any you add to the box on the right will be put in your filing cabinet during your Automatic AOL session. This will increase the time of your session with very busy newsgroups, but your online time will still be greatly reduced. You'll just have to remember to erase the old messages regularly to save disk space.

To visit the Internet Center you click **Internet** on the main Genealogy Forum window.

Surnames Center

The Surnames Center (Fig. 2-14) is another collection of message boards that's organized by surname. But here individual surnames have their own boards, as opposed to the surname boards you can reach from the Quick Start Guide, which groups surnames alphabetically.

The same rules and suggestions discussed earlier apply to these message boards. The only difference is that these message boards are each focused on a single surname, so you will likely find the messages to be more useful than on another board, even though there will be fewer of them.

Search the Forum

Clicking **Search the Forum** on the Genealogy Forum main window opens the Genealogy Search window. When you enter a search term in this window, the program will search the file libraries in the forum. The program does not search the messages. The result is a list of files that contain the search term.

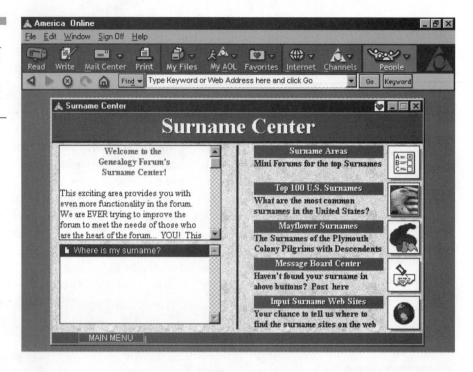

Other Resources

You've now learned about the main areas of the Genealogy Forum. But beyond those areas are all sorts of other useful resources. The following sections are short descriptions of some of these resources.

Genealogy Forum News

In the Genealogy Forum News window, you'll find various announcements, the monthly forum newsletter, schedules for chats and classes, and all the other fast-changing information in the forum. Several genealogy special interest groups (SIGs) like the U.S. Civil War SIG also post monthly newsletters here.

DearMYRTLE Daily Column

A daily column on genealogy topics, DearMYRTLE Daily is always helpful and informative. The DearMYRTLE Daily Column area (Fig. 2-15) not

■■■ ■■■ ■■■ ■■■
Figure 2-15
Myrtle's section of the
Genealogy Forum
offers a daily column
and much more.

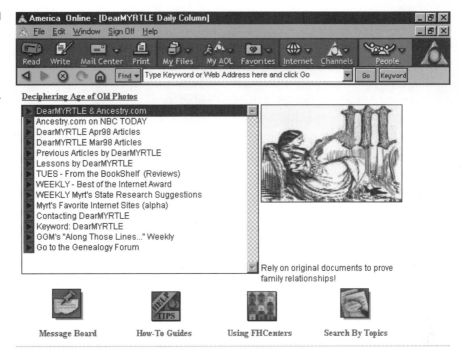

only contains Myrtle's columns but also a message board, a collection of
how-to guides, and much more.

Telephone Search Facilities

The Telephone Search Facilities window gives you access to nine World
Wide Web sites that you can use to track down the phone numbers and
addresses of people. If you discover the existence of a long lost cousin, use
this section to help you track down their address and phone number.

The best place to start your search is with AOL's own switchboard
(http://www.switchboard.com/). Switchboard lets you find people, businesses, Web sites, and e-mail addresses.

Ancestral Seasonings Cookbook

It's time for a tasty finale to your visit to the Genealogy Forum. From the
forum's main window, click **Resources** to go to the Resource Center. Now
look in the menu on the left side of the window, and double click **Ancestral Seasonings** to open the Ancestral Seasonings Cookbook (Fig. 2-16).

In the cookbook, you'll find favorite recipes from other AOL genealogists, many passed down from generation to generation. Like most other areas of the forum, this cookbook has five main sections. But there's a difference. These main sections are:

- Soups, Salads & Appetizers
- Entrees & Main Dishes
- Vegetables & Side Dishes
- Pickles, Preserves & Relishes
- Desserts

The menu on the left also has some interesting headings. How about these: Breads & Pizza, International Recipes, or Grandma's Homemade Remedies. Whether any particular recipe has been handed down through the ages or not, you are sure to find something to please your palate.

Figure 2-16
Looking for a tasty treat after a hard day of genealogical research? Take a look in the Ancestral Seasonings Cookbook.

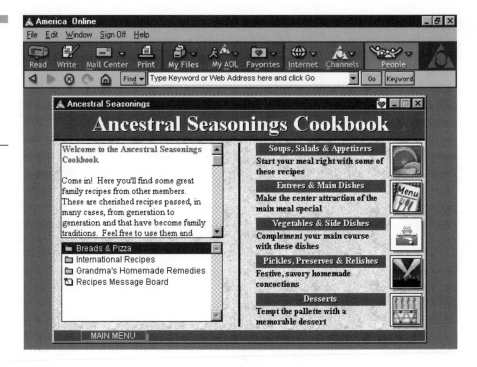

The Staff of the Genealogy Forum

While the Genealogy Forum is full of interesting and useful treasures, by far the most valuable treasure in the forum is the people who staff it.

One of the sysops, GFS Judy, told us: "The Genealogy Forum provides a sense of family. Not only the 'real' relatives you are searching for, but the sense of family you get entering a chat room and being recognized, the information that total strangers go out of their way to type up and e-mail you, the forwarding of problems to others so that everyone can offer a suggestion or just encouragement to keep on going. I am constantly amazed that people who have spent 20 years of their lives, and countless dollars researching their family lines, will freely give out information just to help another researcher and perhaps get a tidbit in return. The materials people upload into the genealogy libraries save me hours of time traveling around the country, as does the Internet access. Computers truly make genealogy a realistic, global project that anyone can join in on regardless of age or income."

The Genealogy Forum is full of wonderful resources for the beginner, intermediate, and advanced genealogist. One of the best features about this forum is the excellent staff of experienced genealogists to help you.

GFL George is the forum leader. GFA Robin, GFA Terry, GFA Beth, and GFA Drew are some of the sysops. There are over 100 staff members in the forum—anyone with GFS at the beginning of their screen name is a Genealogy Forum staff member. A list of the staff, with short bios, can be found in the Welcome Center folder named Volunteers.

GFA Terry is one example. Director of a Mormon Family History Center (FHC), she's the Genealogy Forum expert on FHCs and the Family History Library in Salt Lake City.

"I have been working in the Genealogy Club for years," GFA Terry says. "It started in about 1986 when I joined Q-Link (the first network from the owners of AOL, it was designed for Commodore computers). I worked in the genealogy area of Q-Link as a staff member. When AOL came about and when my husband and I upgraded to an IBM, we joined this network. I was already a staff member on Q-Link (owned by the same company), so it was possible to become one here, too.

"My duties cover many things—I greet the new members, answer some of the questions on the message boards, do some librarian duties as I help make files go live, archive message boards, host meetings, and well, there's a lot to do, but I enjoy it very much."

The network has helped her with her genealogy as well, and she says:

I have made contact with several folks by posting the surnames I was looking for. I even found a distant cousin! This all works on a volunteer princi-
ple—folks helping other folks. One of them lived in Connecticut where I
had ancestors and looked up some information for me. In turn I looked up
some information for her from Georgia. And the genealogy libraries have
helpful text files, too.

Another person you should introduce yourself to is GFL George, the
forum leader. A professional genealogist, George Ferguson has over a
decade's experience with online genealogy and is willing to share, help,
and inform.

"The Genealogy Forum on AOL has been my love and my passion
since its inception in 1988," George said. "With the help of many wonderful and dedicated volunteers we have guided it to the place it is today. My
Great Aunt Gertrude Durham started me on my genealogy work when I
was a boy by presenting me with a ten-generation pedigree chart that was
partially filled. I knew right then my life's work was to fill in the spaces."
George started doing online genealogy research the day after he got his
first modem.

George told me: "The best feature of the America Online Genealogy
Forum would have to be the ability to get 48 people from all over the
country together in one online room and talk about genealogy. It's great
because you don't have to leave the comfort of your own home but you
can get all kinds of questions answered. We also have an outstanding collection of downloadable files. We have programs and utilities for IBM-
compatible systems, Macintosh systems, as well as Apple II systems. We
have hundreds of lineage files, GEDCOM database files, genealogical
records files, tiny tafel files, alphabetic surname files, as well as logs of past
meetings. We have a surnames area where anyone can post a message
about someone they are looking for. We also have message boards that are
designed to exchange information about computer- and noncomputer
genealogical subjects.

"We have started several special interest groups (SIGs), which are becoming quite popular. On different nights we have beginners' classes, an
African-American genealogy SIG, a Southern SIG, and a Scot-Irish SIG. In
the near future we hope to expand these offerings with expanded beginner services, a New England research SIG, and a reunion software users
group."

George Ferguson points out that the online real-time conversations are
a valuable resource. There have been many meetings where somebody

finds a cousin or a possible link. It is also an opportunity to chat with people who have similar interests to you. And you don't have to go out at night or drive into a big city to do it. Also, unlike the big genealogy groups that get together only once every month or so, AOL members can get out and talk almost any night of the week.

"We expect people to come and share the passion for genealogy," George said. "We expect nothing, but hope that everyone will share what they have with the rest of us and have fun doing it. What we find is that people freely give of themselves and that we can have a good time while learning different ways of investigating the past."

Another Forum host, GFH Ranch, said, "Long before I assisted with a chat or had any formal involvement with AOL, I was a regular. For me, personally, the chats and message boards have been very instrumental in meeting cousins, which in turn leads to more sources, more information, and more options for research.

"I had used the genealogy newsgroups but prefer working the break-down of topics that AOL offers. Message boards are broken into portions of the alphabet and geographic locations which dramatically reduces the amount you have to look through to find a possible connection," she added. "Chat sessions are narrowed to geographic areas [as well as offering general and beginner chats] and historical time periods."

Like many others on AOL, she has had good luck finding real information there. "It is especially fun the first time you find a cousin. One time I helped a lady find a missing link because I had an editor's note in a book. And another contact sent me an ancestor's photograph giving me a rare opportunity to share it with my family. I now have trouble remembering all the cousins I've met. Chats focus on families and heritage with a strong sense of helping our brother out. We have folks in Tennessee offering to assist someone in Texas by calling the courthouse or photographing a tombstone."

CHAPTER 3

Other Genealogy Resources on America Online

While the Genealogy Forum is the center of America Online genealogical activity, it isn't the only place you'll want to visit. This chapter takes you on a guided tour of other useful AOL forums like the Adoption Forum, NetNoir (an area dedicated to all things African-American), and Native Sons & Daughters (a forum for Native Americans).

When you visit any of these forums, remember these general guidelines.

- Always read any FAQ or "About" files. These will help you get the most out of the forums and may keep you from embarrassing yourself by being the 300th person to ask a particular question, or otherwise violating the etiquette of the forum.

- Don't be afraid to explore. While organization and planning are the keys to productive genealogical research, chance plays a part, too. We can't possibly cover each of these forums in the depth they deserve—and even if we could, they are always growing and changing. The exact item you need might have been added to a forum since we wrote this.

- Have fun! AOL forums are the products of lots of hard work and dedication. They're also full of interesting surprises.

The Adoption Forum

The Adoption Forum (Keyword: *Adoption*) is designed to provide information, education, and support to anyone who visits. Members known as Community Leaders freely share their experience and expertise, helping visitors to get the most out of the forum.

The forum's main window looks like Fig. 3-1. You'll notice that the layout is similar to the Genealogy Forum's main window, which you saw in Chap. 2.

The Adoption Forum main window has three buttons on the left, leading to the Message Boards, Conference Center, and Forum Libraries. On the right is a menu containing additional forum areas and resources. In addition, the top left corner of the main window is a message area, where short important messages from the forum staff may appear.

The Adoption Forum Message Boards, Conference Center, and Forum Libraries are all similar to their counterparts in the Genealogy Forum. The main difference is, of course, the specific subject matter. As of this writing, there are eight active message boards, with the Adoption Search Board and Search Issues of particular interest to genealogists. In the Conference Center there are nightly chats, with specific topics scheduled for certain nights and times. Previous topics have included Beginning the

Figure 3-1
If adoption is part of
your family history, the
Adoption Forum is a
useful place to visit.

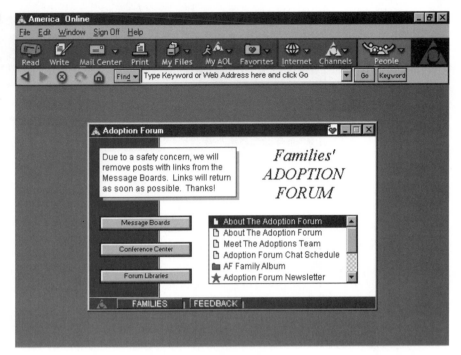

Adoption Process, Fostering Support Group Chat, Touched by Adoption, and similar themes. The Forum Libraries cover Adoption Discussions, which are logs of guest chats and other chat sessions of general interest as well as more general Adoption Information.

In the menu of additional sections and resources, you should be sure to check out the Adoption Forum Newsletter, as well as the Forum Resource Center. The Forum Resource Center (Fig. 3-2) contains useful information like Beginning Search Advice, Sample Information Letters, and the Web Site Request Form. This form allows you to request that the Adoption Forum staff add a link to an existing adoption-related Web site to the collection of links maintained at this site.

NOTE   *Web sites are locations on the World Wide Web (the Web), which is the multimedia portion of the Internet. Chapter 6 has complete information on the Web and Web sites.*

The Forum Resource Center also has separate links to certain major adoption-related Web sites, including the AdoptionNetwork.

Figure 3-2
The Adoption
Forum's Resource
Center contains
useful information for
people searching for
their birth families.

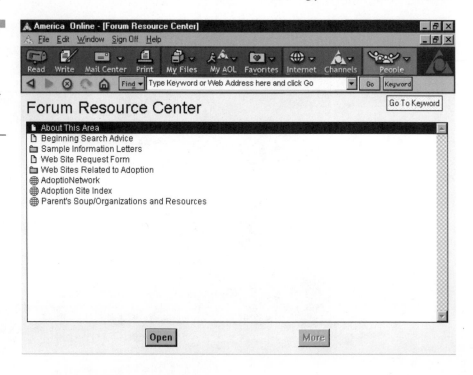

Hispanic Online

Hispanic Online (Keyword: *Hispanic Online*) is a center of Hispanic news, information, and resources on AOL. With a lively design (Fig. 3-3) and connections to Hispanic Magazine and the Hispanic Online Web site, this forum covers all aspects of Hispanic life, including genealogy.

The forum is comprised of six main sections, all of which can be reached by clicking buttons on the Hispanic Online Main Window or by entering the appropriate keyword.

- *Mundo (Keyword:* Mundo*).* News and politics are provided, with links to other AOL and Web resources.

- *Ritmo (Keyword:* Ritmo*).* Arts and entertainment can be found here.

- *Vida (Keyword:* Vida*).* Lifestyles and interests, including Hispanic heritage, make this a definite destination for genealogists.

- *Mercado (Keyword:* Mercado*).* This is an online store for Latino goods and services.

- *Dialogo (Keyword:* Dialogo*).* The interactive section of the forum, this is the place to find chat rooms and message boards.

Figure 3-3
Hispanic Online covers all aspects of Hispanic life, including genealogy.

- *HOL: Web.* A link to HISPANIC Online, this is the Web site (http://www.hisp.com/) of Hispanic Magazine.

One part of the forum for genealogists to visit is Your Hispanic Roots Online (Fig. 3-4). This area features the family histories for thousands of Hispanic surnames, organized into folders alphabetically. While for some surnames the information is limited, for example, "Pablo ABAMEA and Maria were married in May of 1760 at El Sagrario, Chihuahua, Chihuahua, Mexico (IGI, 1984)," for others there is quite an extensive write-up. Be sure to click **More** to see additional surnames in each list.

NOTE   *The material in Your Hispanic Roots Online comes from the Root Search feature that appears regularly in Vista Magazine. You can e-mail the author of the feature, Jose A. de la Torre of Spain, with a request to review a surname that isn't covered in Your Hispanic Roots Online.*

To reach Your Hispanic Roots Online, click **Vida** in the main forum window, then find Your Hispanic Roots Online in the Vida main menu.

Figure 3-4
Your Hispanic Roots
Online contains
information about
hundreds of Hispanic
surnames.

Raices Latinas!

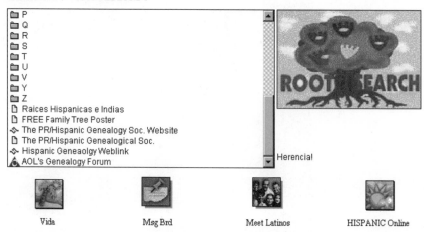

The genealogy resources in the Hispanic Forum don't end with Your Hispanic Roots Online. Explore other sections of Vida, like N. African/ Arab Influences to find additional surnames. And Search Hispanic Online can also produce useful results.

History Forum

The History Forum (Keyword: *History*) is a part of the AOL Research & Learn Channel. It serves primarily to connect members to history resources located in other sections of AOL. As Fig. 3-5 shows, the main window of the forum contains a list of History Resources plus links to a few featured areas or items. Right now, these links include a book on the history of Women's Suffrage and a button that takes you to the History Channel main window on AOL.

You get to the History Forum by clicking **History** in the Research & Learn main window or by using the keyword.

Figure 3-5
The History Forum is primarily a place to connect to historical resources in other parts of AOL.

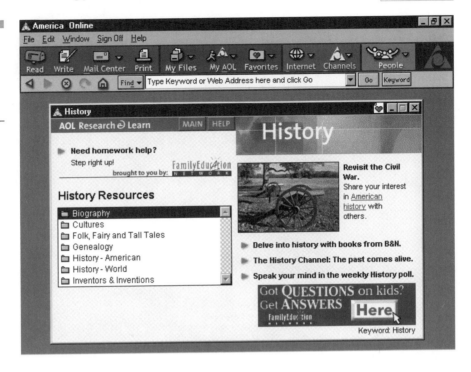

The heart of this forum is the **History Resources** menu. There's a folder for Genealogy, which allows you to search or connect to the Genealogy Forum. The **Biography** menu selection has links to Web sites such as 4000 Years of Women in Science (http://www.astr.ua.edu/4000ws/4000WS.html) and Biography.com (http://www.biography.com/). If one of your ancestors was famous, you may find useful information here. Other potentially useful selections in the **History Resources** menu include Cultures, History, and Inventors & Inventions.

Irish Heritage

If you've got Irish blood, then the Irish Heritage (Keyword: *Irish Heritage*) forum is for you. Once you get to the forum (Fig. 3-6), you'll see that the forum has the usual chat rooms and message boards. But the real goodies are in the four main sections.

Figure 3-6
If you are researching
Irish ancestors, you'll
find lots of informa-
tion at Irish Heritage.

Figure 3-6
If you are researching
Irish ancestors, you'll
find lots of informa-
tion at Irish Heritage.

- *Irish in America.* Celebrate your heritage!
- *Ireland Today.* News from the source
- *Culture and History.* Kings, poets, and more
- *Folklore and Legends.* A look at mystic Eire

We suggest you start your research by clicking **Irish in America**. The menu in this window (Fig. 3-7) gives you a chance to do things like visiting the Great Hall of the Clans (which contains the history of over 140 Scottish clans) and visiting Web sites like the Irish Family History Foundation (http://www.mayo-ireland.ie/roots.htm) and IRLGEN: Tracing Your Irish Ancestors (http://www.bess.tcd.ie/roots_ie.htm).

In the Irish in America window there's also the opportunity to Share your family's immigration story. This button actually takes you to the Tell Us Your Story forum, which is covered later in this chapter.

After returning to the main forum window, you should click Culture and History. Not only can you get a photographic tour of Ireland, but you can also study the language of your people in the Irish Gaelic Learning Center, learn about The Potato Famine, explore Celtic Mythology & Legend, or subscribe to the Irish Heritage forum newsletter.

Figure 3-7
Irish-Americans will
find lots to interest
them in this window.

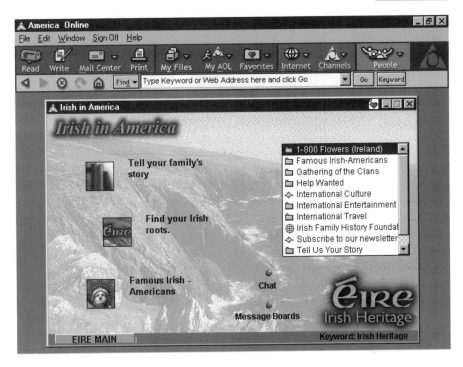

JEWISH.COMMunity

JEWISH.COMMunity (Keyword: *Jewish*) is another AOL forum organized around a particular ethnic group. The forum covers virtually any
topic of interest to Jewish people: education, culture, heritage, religion,
and more. The JEWISH.COMMunity is a fully equipped forum with
chat rooms, message boards, and download areas. In addition, there are
features like This Day (which relates facts and trivia for this day in history), News, Classifieds, even a Matchmaker, all just a click away from the
forum's main window (Fig. 3-8).

You can find genealogical information in various sections of the
forum. Arts & Culture is one obvious place to visit. Here you'll find information on Jewish Museums and Cultural Organizations (Fig. 3-9), as well
as the Arts & Culture message board.

Another place to look for information is the Family section. In particular, the **Family Web Links** menu option has links to JewishGen: The
Home of Jewish Genealogy (http://www.jewishgen.org/), Stars of David
International, Inc. Jewish Adoption Information Exchange (http://www
.starsofdavid.org/), and other resources.

Figure 3-8
JEWISH.COMMunity
strives to be a
complete Jewish
community in
cyberspace.

Figure 3-9
Come to Cultural
Organizations to get
contact and
background
information on
various Jewish
organizations,
including
JEWISHGEN:
Association of Jewish
Genealogical Societies.

Last but not least, the Jewish Community Newsletter sometimes carries articles on genealogical topics. You can subscribe for free and back issues are available.

Language Dictionaries & Resources

If you run into foreign words or phrases in your research, you can probably find a translation in the Language Dictionaries & Resources forum (Keyword: *Foreign Dictionary*). This forum, shown in Fig. 3-10, features dictionaries for dozens of languages, sound clips, and translation aids.

If you're interested in a European language, you'll want to click **Translate words from—or into—almost any European language**. When you do, you'll go to the Web site of EURODICAUTOM (http://www2.echo .lu/edic/). The tools at this site let you translate between ten languages, with about 40 categories (from Agriculture to Zoology) to help keep the search focused.

Figure 3-10

Foreign words or phrases need not interfere with your research, thanks to the Language Dictionaries & Resources forum.

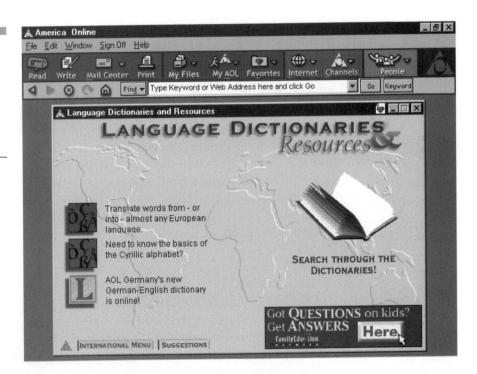

Another interesting button is labeled Need to know the basics of the Cyrillic alphabet? (http://www.friends-partners.org/newfriends/cyrillic/russian.alphabet.html). It takes you to a Web site that teaches you how to pronounce the basics of the Cyrillic language. But the main attraction in the Language Dictionaries & Resources forum remains the extensive collection of online foreign dictionaries.

The Dictionaries by language area is huge and diverse. Need help with Welsh? No problem. Zulu or Xhosa? Ditto. Chinese or Chechen? Afrikaans or Australian Aboriginal? You're covered. Many of the actual dictionaries reside on the Internet, but this area is a central switching station for finding the language dictionaries you need.

Native Americans

Here's a good example of the way things change online. When we first wrote this chapter, AOL had a forum named Native Sons & Daughters, which was dedicated to Native Americans, their culture, tribes/nations, and more. By the time we were doing our final review of this chapter, Native Sons & Daughters was gone! It had become part of the Ethnicity forum (Keyword: *Ethnicity*). The Ethnicity forum (Fig. 3-11) is a common area for resources from numerous ethnic groups as well as a central location from which you can jump to forums like Genealogy, Jewish Community, and NetNoir.

You get to the Native American material by clicking **Ethnicity Communities** (Fig. 3-12) in the main Ethnicity window. There you will find Native American Boards discussing current events and history, plus several file libraries such as Native America Stories (both folklore and family history), Native American Treaties (text files), Native American Histories (sorted by nation), and graphics in Native American Arts, Crafts, and Personal Photos.

Tawodi's Native American Genealogy Help (http://members.aol.com/tawodi/index.html) Web site is a great place if you are just starting out in Native American genealogy. It starts with a basic guide to researching Native American roots and progresses from there.

Tawodi's site is also part of two Web rings: the Native Peoples' Ring, and the Native Genealogy Web Ring. Web rings are groups of Web sites united by their subject matter. Each site in a ring has connections to the sites before and after it, so you can move easily from one to another without straying from the sites that make up the ring. Web rings help people like

Figure 3-11
You can find Native
American information
among the ethnic
resources gathered in
the Ethnicity forum.

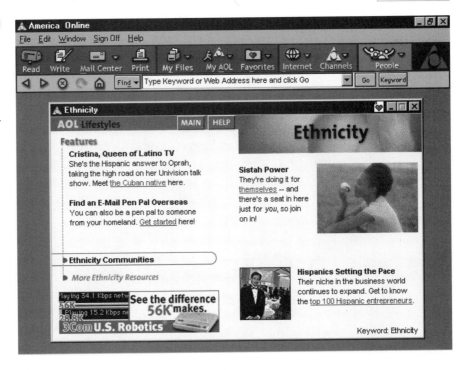

Figure 3-12
This window gives
you access to Native
American message
boards and file
libraries.

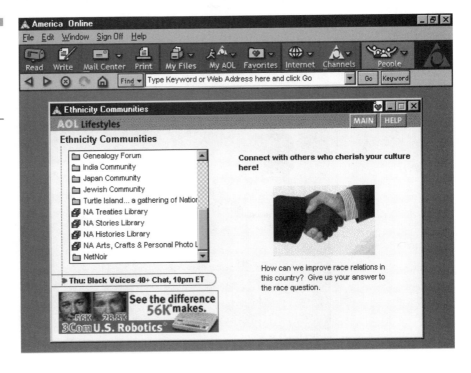

us, because they unite sites dealing with subjects we're interested in. They help the owners of the Web sites because connection with a ring will bring more people to the site.

Another Native American resource is the Native American Genealogy Home Page (http://members.aol.com/bbbenge/front.html), the official home page of the AOL Native American Genealogy Group. This site has a large collection of genealogy materials, all dealing specifically with Native Americans. From Native American Bookstores and Maps (a page of 60+ links to online bookstores and maps) to Frontier Press Bookstore, to the Native American Locator (a set of clickable maps for locating former tribal lands), this site is sure to figure prominently in your research.

NetNoir

NetNoir—The Black Network is the place to start your research if you have African-American ancestors. This forum (Fig. 3-13) bills itself as Your

Figure 3-13
NetNoir is a great resource for information on African-American ancestors.

Home for Black Interactive Culture and Entertainment. As the figure shows, this forum supports a wide range of interests, from the serious to the frivolous. You can reach NetNoir with the Keyword: *NetNoir.*

The primary genealogical resource at NetNoir is the Genealogy Boards area. To get there, click **Black Boards** on the main forum window, then choose **Genealogy Boards**. This takes you to a set of genealogy-related topics (five when we wrote this). From here you can do all the usual message board activities. If you are looking for information on specific surnames, try the Genealogy & Kinfolk (Fig. 3-14) message board. You can post queries on this board with a reasonable hope that someone can assist you. The other topics in this board can also be helpful.

Beyond the Genealogy Boards, there's plenty of general information, but you'll need to do some digging to turn up more material directly related to genealogy. Your best bet may be to ask around in some of the chats and message boards.

Figure 3-14
NetNoir contains its own genealogy message boards.

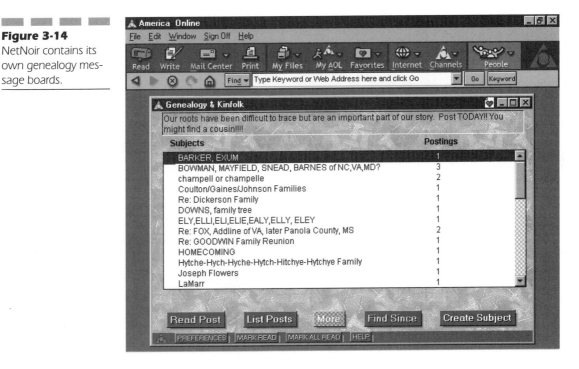

AOL Online Campus

Another AOL feature you should explore is the Online Campus (Keyword: *Online Campus,* then click **Course Catalog**). In this forum (Fig. 3-15) you can sign up for all sorts of courses, some free (except for connect charges), some with small fees (around $20) required. If you take a look in the **Humanities/History** menu, you'll find classes like Genealogy & Family History Centers. These courses are for new and experienced users who want to learn more about the genealogy resources available as well as the LDS (Latter Day Saints) family history centers.

Online interaction with the instructor can help you solve specific research problems and acquaint you in detail with resources available from the Salt Lake Family History Library. To join the class, sign on at the appointed time and go to the assigned chat room. The instructor will present this class's material, and the students will ask questions. Each session lasts about two hours.

Figure 3-15

For a small fee, you can even take online genealogy classes.

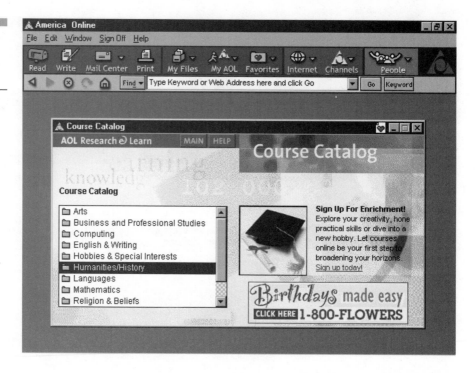

Royalty

If your family tree springs from the United Kingdom, you should visit the Royalty forum (Keyword: *Royalty*). This forum is dedicated to the British Royal family, although it does have some information on Irish and Chinese rulers as well. If you look at the Royalty forum main window (Fig. 3-16), you can see that the forum has four regular areas and two special sections. The regular areas are:

- *Royal Chat.* Scheduled chat sessions on relevant topics
- *Messages.* A message board with more than 40 royalty-related topics, plus a pen pal finder
- *Royal Info.* Information on Diana, Princess of Wales; Royal movies; Majestic Quotes; the forum library; and links to royalty Web sites
- *Newsletter.* The Royalty newsletter

Figure 3-16
Do you have royal blood in your veins? If so, come visit the Royalty forum.

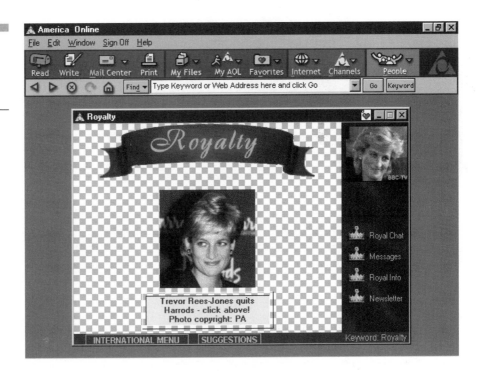

The leftmost of the two special sessions can change daily. Click the image in the center of the Royalty window to see what this topic of the day is all about. The other special section is currently dedicated to Princess Diana. Click her photo to open a miniforum dedicated to the Princess of Wales.

The Royalty Info section of the Royalty site is probably the best source of genealogical information in this forum. Click **Royal Info** in the main window to get here. If you scroll to the end of the **Royalty Info** menu, you'll come across a dozen or so links to Royalty-related Web sites. Two of those links are for genealogy sites covering the Royal family.

Royal Genealogies—Menu is a site (http://ftp.cac.psu.edu/~saw/royal/royalgen.html) containing a version of the ROYAL92.GED. Come here (Fig. 3-17) or go to the unrelated Directory of Royal Genealogical Data (http://www.dcs.hull.ac.uk/public/genealogy/royal/). At either site, you'll get a healthy dose of Royal family genealogy.

Figure 3-17
AOL makes the World Wide Web's royalty information easy to get to. The Royalty forum points you to the best sites.

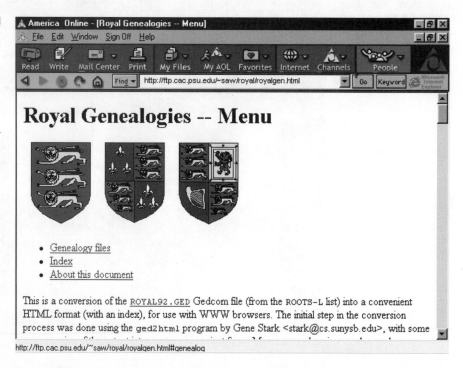

Rev War

Rev War (Keyword: *Rev War*) is AOL's forum for reenactors, historians, and enthusiasts of the American Revolutionary War. It's also a great place to start when you are researching ancestors who fought in, or were affected by, the war. Figure 3-18 shows the Rev War forum's main window, with buttons for the three major sections of the forum: the Rev War Message Boards, Rev War Archives, and Rev War on the Net!

To begin your exploration of this forum, click **Rev War Archives**. You'll be treated to an extensive, three-part history of the Revolutionary War as well as file archives. The Rev War Photo Archive contains over 40 paintings, drawings, and cartoons related to the war. If you are more interested in words than pictures, the Rev War Text File Archive offers a variety of files you may find useful in your own research.

To get other Revolutionary War information, check out the World Wide Web. On the main forum window, click **Rev War on the Net**! When you do, you'll find a collection of links to a list of Revolutionary War Web sites. While most of the links are oriented toward historical

Figure 3-18

Revolutionary War historians, enthusiasts, and reenactors all hang out in the Rev War forum.

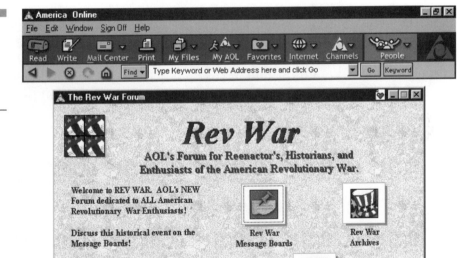

Figure 3-19
The Rev War Message
Boards can give you
answers you couldn't
get elsewhere in the
forum.

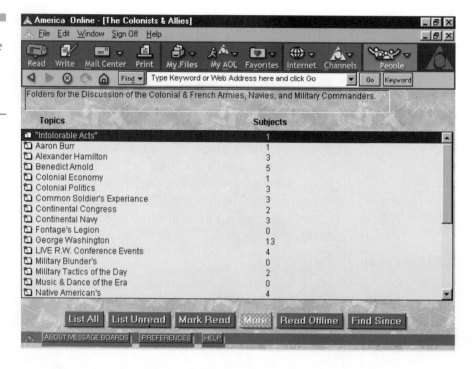

reenactment, some are of use to genealogists. Sites like the Society for American Archaeology (http://www.saa.org/) or the American Revolutionary War Home Page (http://www.ccs.neu.edu/home/bcortez/revwar/) can be helpful in your research.

If you couldn't find the information you need elsewhere in the forum, you may be able to get the answers to your questions by posting a message to the Revolutionary War experts who visit the Rev War forum. Return to the main forum window, then click **Rev War Message Boards** to exchange messages on topics like The British & Hessians or The Colonists & Allies (Fig. 3-19).

Tell Us Your Story—The American Immigration Experience

Is your family a family of immigrants? Most of ours are. If your family did immigrate to the United States, then you should certainly check out Tell Us Your Story—The American Immigration Experience. Use (Keyword: *Tell Us*) to reach this forum. Tell Us Your Story—The American Immigration Experience (Fig. 3-20) has four main areas for you to visit.

- *Immigration Stories.*   Tales of how our ancestors came to this country
- *Stories.*   More tales of immigration, categorized by country of origin
- *Ellis Island.*   A Web site for the Statue of Liberty—Ellis Island Foundation, Inc.
- *Fact of the Day.*   Interesting tidbits of facts from forum members and others

Start your tour with Immigration Stories. Click **Read the stories of America's families** to get here. This area features chat rooms and message boards, as well as a library of historic pictures you can download. In the center of the window you'll find a story with genealogically significant words or phrases converted into links to additional information. Of the six topics in this window, the one we find most interesting is called Find Your Family! To get there, go to the Immigration Stories window, then click **Where is your family today?** When you do, AOL will display the Find Your Family! window shown in Fig. 3-21.

Figure 3-20

Share your tales of the family migration to America in Tell Us Your Story.

Figure 3-21
Use this window
as your gateway
to genealogical
information for the
continents your
ancestors came from.

The point of the Find Your Family! window is to help you trace your ancestors geographically. Click the changing picture for the continent your ancestors came from to see an extensive list of AOL forums and Web sites you can use to further your research. Each continent has not only a list like this but also a message board you can use for queries or other such activities. Wherever your family came from, you are sure to find some worthwhile information in Find Your Family!

The last stop on this guided tour is the Ellis Island Web site at (http://www.ellisisland.org/index.html). While this isn't located on AOL, the site is a great resource, and it is featured on the Tell Us Your Story main window. Click **Ellis Island** to go to this window. As the gateway through which many immigrants flowed, the island, now a museum, is a historical artifact. Figure 3-22 shows the Web site's home page. Make sure that you spend some time exploring this site. You'll learn about the American Immigrant Wall of Honor®, where you can honor your immigrant ancestors for a fee. Right now, the minimum fee is $100.

Figure 3-22

The Ellis Island Web site allows you to search for ancestors who immigrated to the United States through this facility.

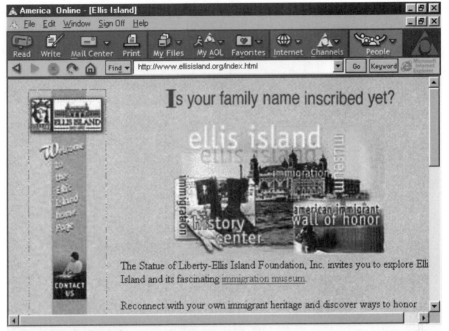

http://www.ellisisland.org/who.html

War Between the States— The Civil War Forum

Wars generate a lot of documents, which makes them useful for genealogists. The Civil War is a perfect example. With all the troops involved, and all of the records generated by the military bureaucracies, the chances are good that you'll find an ancestor in the records somewhere.

War Between the States—The Civil War forum (Keyword: *Civil War*), is a great place to start your search. The forum (Fig. 3-23) is full of historic artwork plus solid documentation about the war and the people who fought in it. The four main areas of the forum are:

■ *Mason-Dixon Line Chat Room.*   Scheduled chats on such subjects as Civil War myths and trivia

■ *Civil War Information Center.*   A collection of resources for researchers, collectors, and reenactors, including a genealogy chat, advice on researching Civil War ancestors, and a service you can hire to do the job for you

Figure 3-23

If your roots trace to
the American Civil War,
this forum could have
just the information
you are looking for.

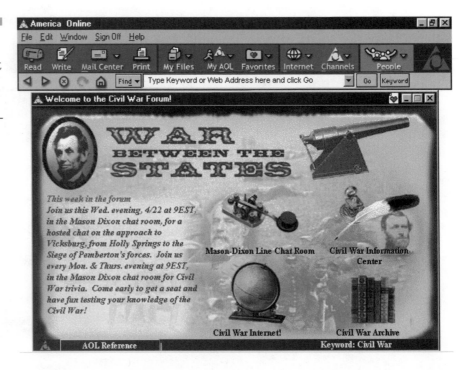

■ *Civil War Archives.* The forum's downloadable file archives, including
lots of photographs from the time of the war as well as from present-
day reenactments of battles

■ *Civil War Internet!* Links to Web-based resources for historians as well
as for reenactors

While there is plenty of good stuff in this forum, the place to start
your research is definitely the Civil War Information Center. Just click
the pen and ink graphic in the main forum window to get there. This
area consists of a list of resources (Fig. 3-24) plus buttons for the Camp
Chase Gazette and the Fall Creek Suttlery, two sites for reenactors.

Within the resource list, the Civil War History and Research folder is
particularly interesting. Inside you'll find another list of resources,
including the Civil War Genealogy Board, a folder full of tips on
Researching Civil War Ancestors, and contact information on the Battlefields Revisited Genealogy Service, a company you can pay to research
your Civil War ancestors for you.

Figure 3-24
The Civil War Informa-
tion Center is a partic-
ularly rich source for
genealogists.

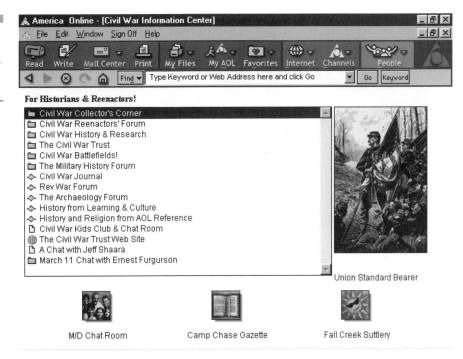

For Historians & Reenactors!

- Civil War Collector's Corner
- Civil War Reenactors' Forum
- Civil War History & Research
- The Civil War Trust
- Civil War Battlefields!
- The Military History Forum
- Civil War Journal
- Rev War Forum
- The Archaeology Forum
- History from Learning & Culture
- History and Religion from AOL Reference
- Civil War Kids Club & Chat Room
- The Civil War Trust Web Site
- A Chat with Jeff Shaara
- March 11 Chat with Ernest Furgurson

Union Standard Bearer

M/D Chat Room   Camp Chase Gazette   Fall Creek Suttlery

While the Civil War Information Center is definitely the place to start, don't forget to look into the Civil War Archives. The Civil War Text Archive includes copies of soldiers' letters that have survived from the war, regimental histories, and background information on life during the war. The Civil War Battles & Bios Archive folder has more than 20 biographies from the period. And the National Archive Civil War Photos Archive contains exactly that, scans of Civil War photographs from the National Archives.

3

Genealogy on the Internet

If you thought America Online was a rich source of genealogy resources, wait until you get serious about the Internet (the Net). AOL is big (heck, it's huge) but the Net is immense. Sometimes it seems like every bit of human knowledge is available on the Net (someday it probably will be). This makes the Net an ideal place to do genealogical research, except for one thing: the Internet is a vast sea of chaos. Incredible resources are out there, somewhere. That's what this section of Genealogy Online is all about, pointing you to the best genealogy resources on the Net and teaching you how to use them. An added bonus is that you can get to all these resources through America Online's Internet connections: e-mail, Web browser, FTP, and Usenet connections. So you're always only a few mouse clicks away from the organized, user-friendly environment of AOL. The three Internet services of the most use in your genealogical researches will be mailing lists, newsgroups, and the World Wide Web. Each of these has its own chapter in this section, so turn the page and get ready to take advantage of the vast genealogical resources of the Internet.

CHAPTER 4

Genealogy Mailing Lists

Electronic mailing lists are electronic discussion groups based on e-mail messages. All subscribers can send e-mail to the list and receive e-mail from the list. Messages sent to the mailing list get forwarded to everyone who subscribes to the list. Replies to messages from the list get sent to the list, where they get forwarded to all participants. And so it goes.

Mailing lists can be completely automated, with a program taking care of subscribing people to the list, forwarding messages, and removing people from the list. Or humans can get into the loop, handling any and all of the mailing list functions that programs can do. Such moderated mailing lists could have restricted membership (only adoptees for example), or the humans could review each incoming message before it gets distributed, preventing inappropriate material from making it onto the list.

There are plenty of mailing lists that focus specifically on genealogy. In addition, there are many more lists that, while not specifically for genealogists, cover topics of interest to genealogists such as ethnic groups or historic events, which can tell you more about the movements of your possible ancestors.

America Online, with its built-in e-mail program, makes it easy for you to participate in mailing lists.

NOTE *Throughout this chapter you'll find references to newsgroups and Web sites. If you don't know anything about these yet, don't worry. This is just an example of how interconnected the genealogy resources on the Internet can be. You will learn everything you need to know about newsgroups and Web sites in coming chapters.*

Mailing Lists and America Online

To use America Online with mailing lists, you need to know how to use electronic mail, how to send and receive messages and attachments. Fortunately, e-mail is easy to use, and most people who are on AOL already know how to use it. If you are an e-mail veteran, skip right down to Automatic AOL. If you are new to e-mail, or just want to brush up on the subject, keep reading.

All your e-mail activities start in the America Online Mail Center (Keyword: *Mail Center*). You can reach the Mail Center with the keyword, or by clicking the **Mail Center** button on the toolbar. As Fig. 4-1 shows,

Figure 4-1
The America Online Mail Center is your gateway to dozens of genealogical mailing lists.

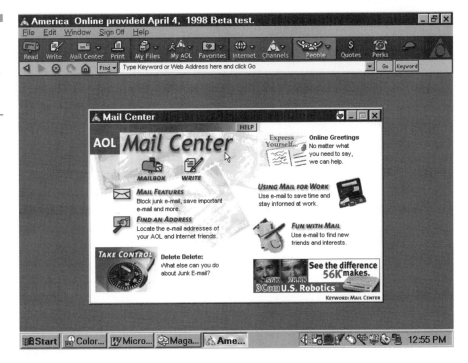

the Mail Center is the place to go to read or send e-mail as well as look up e-mail addresses, send greetings, adjust your e-mail settings, and so on.

As you'll soon learn, to subscribe to a mailing list you need to send an e-mail message to the right e-mail address. To find mailing lists you can subscribe to, you can use keyword *Mailing List.* Later in this chapter, you'll find a short list that will give you some genealogy mailing lists to get started with, and the next few paragraphs will tell you how to do it.

Sending E-mail

Say you want to subscribe to the ROOTS-L genealogy mailing list, and you know that you need to send e-mail to roots-l-request@rootsweb.com, with the message *subscribe,* to join the list. Here is how you do it.

1. Click the **Compose Mail** icon in the Mail Center. The icon is labeled Compose Mail and looks like a piece of paper with a pencil. Clicking this icon causes AOL to open the Compose Mail window.

2. In the **To**: box, type roots-l-request@rootsweb.com.

3. In the **Message** box, which is the large box located below the Subject box, type *subscribe*.

4. Click the **Spell Check** button to be sure there are no typos, then click the **Send** button on the top left side of the Compose Mail window. This causes AOL to send your e-mail on its way.

Reading E-mail

Reading e-mail is even easier than sending it. When you start an AOL session, you go through the usual log on procedure, then end up at the Welcome window. In the Welcome window you'll see the icon for the Mail Center, as well as on the toolbar. If you have new e-mail, the icon will look like a mailbox with a letter sticking out of it, and the words *Mail Center* are replaced by the words *You Have Mail.* If not, the icon will look like an envelope, and the caption will be *Mail Center.*

NOTE *If your computer has a sound card and speakers set up properly, you'll already know that you have mail, because AOL announces the presence of new mail with a "You've got mail" message in a pleasant masculine voice.*

To actually read your new mail, click the **Mail Center** icon. AOL will open a window with a list of new messages for you to read. Select the message you want to read by clicking on it, then open the message by clicking the **Read** button (or you can just double click the message). Under Windows 95, you can also double click the icon of a message to open it.

The message appears in a large, scrollable box on the right side of the window with three buttons, Reply, Forward, and Reply to All, on the left. If the message is too large for AOL's mail reader to handle, you'll have a couple of additional buttons underneath the message window (more on this in the section on the ROOTS-L mailing list). That's all there is to it.

Automatic AOL

If you're like me (Bill), you find it hard not to check your e-mail regularly, like hourly. But it is a pain having to manually log onto AOL several times a day. America Online has the perfect solution for compulsive mail readers like me, Automatic AOL.

Automatic AOL lets your computer automatically connect to AOL, check your mail, send any pending e-mail messages, and download files or newsgroup messages. Once you set up Automatic AOL, you can just sit back and let the computer do all the work. You don't even have to be in the same room—they are totally automatic.

To set up Automatic AOL you need to click the **Mail Center** button on the toolbar, then select **Set up Automatic AOL** (Automatic AOLs). This gives you a window with a list of features as shown in Fig. 4-2.

Now click the **Automatic AOL** icon in the lower right corner of the window to begin setting up a session. The first time you set up an Automatic AOL, the Automatic AOL Walk-Through window appears. Your best bet is to click **Continue** to let AOL walk you through the process of setting up a session. If you've done this before or are more daring, you can click **Expert Setup** to set everything at once, without help.

Assuming you stuck with the walk-through, you'll come to a series of windows, each with a specific question on setting up Automatic AOL. Each question is explained in a window, with pros and cons of each possible answer. Continue answering questions, and you'll eventually come to the Screen Names window.

Figure 4-2

Automatic AOL helps you save money by automatically connecting to AOL, downloading e-mail, newsgroup posts, and specified files, then immediately disconnecting from the system.

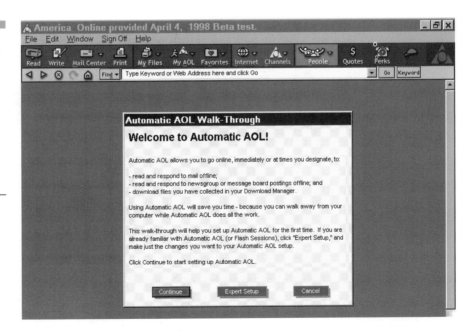

In the Screen Names window, you tell AOL which of your five allowable screen names this Automatic AOL should act on. Again, everything is fully explained in the window—just read the text and make your choices.

After the Screen Names window you get to set the schedule for your Automatic AOL. In the windows that appear, select the days of the week and hours of the day that you want Automatic AOL to occur.

You can also set up Automatic AOL so that they don't occur automatically and instead only happen when you click **Activate Automatic AOL Now** on the **Mail** menu.

As mentioned earlier, the Expert window (Fig. 4-3) lets you set up your sessions without the step-by-step help in the walk-through. Click the **Expert Setup** button to get here.

Once you've completed setting up Automatic AOL, you can read any incoming mail and compose outgoing messages while offline. To do so, click **Mail** on the AOL main menu, then click **Read Incoming Flash-Mail** or **Compose Mail** as appropriate.

When composing mail to send via Automatic AOL you need to click **Send Later** once you finish composing your message. Any message you compose this way can be sent by Automatic AOL. You can see which messages will be sent in the next regular or Automatic AOL session by clicking **Mail** on the AOL main menu, then click **Read Outgoing FlashMail**.

Figure 4-3

The Expert window lets you customize Automatic AOL quickly, once you understand how it works.

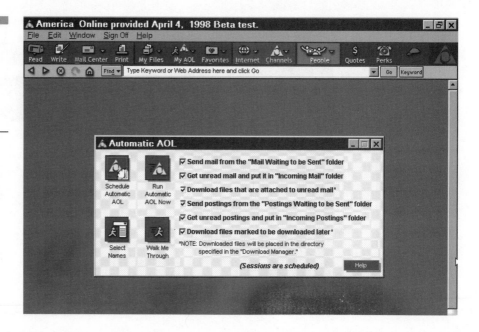

Now that you know how to send and receive e-mail using AOL's mail program, you're ready to learn about one of the best genealogy mailing lists in existence, ROOTS-L.

An In-Depth Visit to ROOTS-L

Imagine a worldwide, never ending conversation about genealogy, where novices and experts exchange help, information, ideas, and gossip. Now imagine that this conversation is conducted by electronic mail (e-mail), so you don't have to worry about missing anything. You've just imagined ROOTS-L, the grandparent of genealogy mailing lists on the Internet.

ROOTS-L has spawned entire generations of newer genealogy mailing lists, some large, some small. But this is the original. The list has a home page on the World Wide Web (you'll learn how to visit Web sites in a coming chapter) at http://www.rootsweb.com/roots-l (see Fig. 4-4).

In 1997, over 7000 people were subscribed to ROOTS-L. To subscribe, you need two things.

Figure 4-4
This Web site contains archived messages from ROOTS-L, the original genealogy mailing list on the Internet.

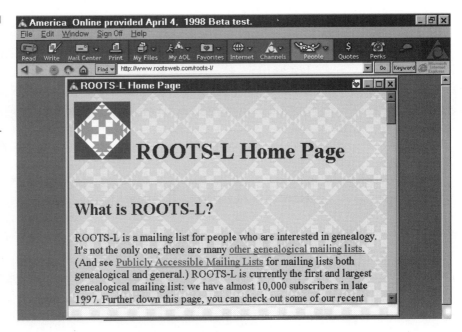

1. You need a large e-mail box to hold the volume of messages that you'll get.

2. You need to send e-mail to roots-l-request@rootsweb.com with the message SUBSCRIBE. Don't include anything else in the message—no signature block, no name or address—just the word *subscribe*.

NOTE   *If you ever decide to leave the list, you unsubscribe by sending e-mail to roots-l-request@rootsweb.com, with the message UNSUBSCRIBE. Don't include anything else in the message—no signature block, no name or address—just the word* unsubscribe.

ROOTS-L Goals

The ROOTS-L mailing list has several clearly established goals.

■ To provide subscribers with a way to communicate and request information about genealogy (family history)

■ To provide a forum for communications, since there is no physical location for all the subscribers to congregate and exchange ideas (This means that ROOTS-L is open to people from all over the world and not just North America.)

■ To be a means of keeping informed of activities taking place in the genealogical community (However, be aware that rumors spread as fast as news.)

■ To be a meeting place for those who wish to learn how to find information concerning their own families and share what they have learned

■ To help people learn to spell the word *genealogy* (!)

Some ROOTS-L Rules

■ Memorize this rule: messages to people go to roots-l@rootsweb.com; commands to programs go to roots-l-request@rootsweb.com.

■ The list is not a place to refight old wars or discuss religion or politics.

■ Advertising or selling a product is not, in general, acceptable. You can, however, post a new-product announcement.

- Make sure that you spell the word *genealogy* correctly in all your messages.
- Don't post messages longer than about 100 lines unless you are sure they will be of very general interest.
- Don't include a *surname signature* (e.g., "Searching POWELL, SPENCER, BEEMAN, ABBOT") in your messages. These are lists of surnames that appear at the end of every message some people send. The surnames play havoc with the lists archive searches, so don't use them.
- Don't post copyrighted material like newspaper articles or e-mail messages sent to you by other people.

Communicating with People and Programs

We covered this rule earlier in the chapter, but people tend to get confused about this, so here are more details. If you're already sure you know where to send messages to people subscribed to ROOTS-L, as opposed to sending commands to the software at ROOTS-L, you can skip the rest of this section.

It can be hard to remember the distinction between the list server that runs a mailing list, and the list itself. This problem is common to most mailing lists. The list server gets all the commands: subscribe, unsubscribe, send me digests, etc. The list gets messages you want to send to other people. For ROOTS-L, messages addressed to roots-l@rootsweb.com go to the mailing list. Messages addressed to roots-l-request@rootsweb.com get posted on the list for all to see. Whenever you subscribe to a mailing list, you'll get a welcome message that tells you the address of the server and the address of the list.

So if you wanted to request help finding information about your Aunt Tilly, you would send your message to roots-l@rootsweb.com. If you wanted to request a copy of the Roots Surname List (described in the next section), you would send your message to roots-l-request@rootsweb.com.

Available Files and Databases

ROOTS-L has tons of files and databases, and you can get these by e-mailing the appropriate commands to the list server that runs ROOTS-L. You can search the ROOTS-L Library for everything from a fabulous collection devoted to obtaining vital records, to useful tips for beginners, to book lists from the Library of Congress, and more. Some of the available files are:

- *The Roots Surname List (RSL).*   A list of over 350,000 surnames and contact information for the 50,000 people researching those surnames
- *The Roots Location List (RLL).*   A list of locations of special interest to individual researchers, along with contact information for those researchers
- *U.S. Civil War Units.*   A file containing information about the military units that served in the United States Civil War
- *The Irish-Canadian List.*   A list of Irish immigrants who settled in Canada, including (where available) dates and locations
- *Books We Own.*   Books and other genealogical resources owned by Internet genealogists are found here. The owners are willing to look up information in them, under certain conditions.

When you subscribe to ROOTS-L, you receive a long welcome message that tells you everything you need to know to get started with ROOTS-L, including how to ask the list server to e-mail files to you.

NOTE   *You can also retrieve files yourself by going to the ROOTS-L Web site and browsing for them.*

Putting ROOTS-L to Work

Now that you are subscribed to ROOTS-L, and know all the rules, it is time to learn how to put the list server to work. You can control your subscription from your e-mail program. But you must remember that you can only control your subscription from the same e-mail account with which you subscribed in the first place. That means you need to use the same AOL screen name you subscribed with. The commands you send will be processed automatically by the list processor—if you remember to send them to roots-l-request@rootsweb.com. If you send your commands to roots-l@rootsweb.com, you'll just succeed in irritating the volunteers who screen all messages before they get posted, and your commands won't get processed.

When you first subscribe to ROOTS-L, you are subscribed in *digest* mode. That means once or twice a day you will receive a large message from ROOTS-L containing a list of all the messages that have been posted to the list since the last digest message. For each topic, there is a topic number, a subject, and who posted it. Figure 4-5 shows a piece of a typical digest message.

Digests from ROOTS-L tend to be larger than America Online's e-mail program can view. Instead of showing the whole message, AOL displays only the first part of the message. A copy of the entire message is converted into a text file and stored in AOL's download folder on your computer. From there, it's up to you to open the file with a word processor or text editor and read the messages. Here's how you do it on a Microsoft Windows 95 system.

1. When the AOL e-mail program shows you the message, click the **Download File** button to load the entire message onto your computer. Make a note of the name which AOL (or the sender) assigns to the file.

2. Using Windows Explorer, find the Download folder under the AOL40 folder. (If you are using a different version of the AOL software, this folder will have a different name, like AOL30 for version 3.0 of the AOL software.)

Figure 4-5

ROOTS-L normally delivers all messages together in a digest message.

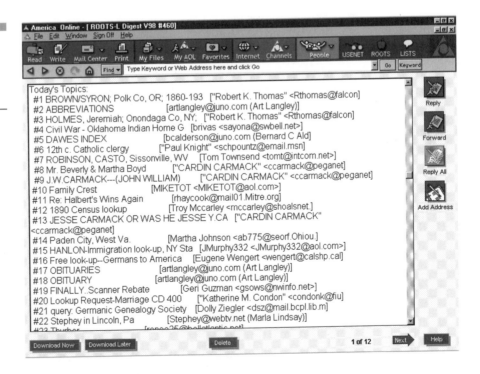

3. Double click the icon that corresponds to the message text file you want to read. That will open the file using Windows Notepad, a text editor.

You can get around this work by telling the list server to give you each message separately by switching to *mail mode* or *index mode*. Instructions on how to switch modes are included in the welcome messages you receive when you join ROOTS-L.

In index mode, all you'll get will be message subject lines with associated message numbers. If you see a message that interests you, send e-mail to roots-l-request@rootsweb.com. In this message, the subject should be ARCHIVE. In the body of the message, you list the numbers of the messages you want to read, say messages numbered 65321 and 65400. The body of your message would look like this:

```
get messages/65321
get messages/65400
```

The commands must be in lowercase, and you must use this slash /, not this one \. And you can only include one request per line. So a complete message to the list server asking for the full text of messages 65321 and 65400 would look similar to Fig. 4-6.

Figure 4-6

An e-mail message requesting the full text of two messages posted to ROOTS-L.

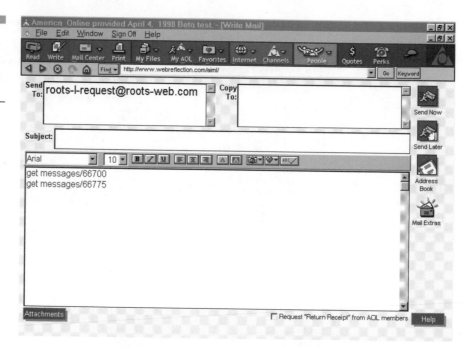

Losing Contact with ROOTS-L

It's possible that you'll stop receiving messages from ROOTS-L even though you didn't unsubscribe. There are two likely causes for this problem.

- America Online could be having trouble with its e-mail server. Any service that is growing as fast as AOL can have occasional problems. However, the company has made huge efforts to eliminate these problems. If all your e-mail has stopped coming, and not just mail from ROOTS-L, this could be the cause.

- You are using a different AOL screen name than the one you used to subscribe to ROOTS-L. Since each AOL screen name has its own mailbox, all the ROOTS-L messages you are missing are probably sitting in that other mailbox, waiting for you to log on with that screen name.

If all else fails, just subscribe to ROOTS-L again. That should get the messages flowing for you.

Other Genealogy Mailing Lists

Once you've mastered how ROOTS-L works, you're ready to sample other mailing lists. Over the next several pages, we've listed just a sampling of mailing lists related to genealogy that you can join. When you see the term *gatewayed* or *mirrored* to <<some Usenet group>>, it means the messages from the list are copied to the corresponding Usenet group, so you have two ways to access it. You could subscribe to them via Usenet (see Chap. 5), but before you subscribe, e-mail if you want to audition them.

Not all mailing lists run on a list server. Some are managed *by hand,* so to speak. This means there is some person out there who receives all the messages, then forwards them to all the list subscribers. You subscribe to such lists by sending a politely worded message to an address such as afrigeneas-request@drum.ncsc.org. The message will go to the list owner, who will read it when he or she has the time, then add you to the list as soon as they can (assuming they decide they want to add you to their list).

When you see the word *request* in the subscription information for one of the following mailing lists, assume that your message is going to a real live person, not a machine. Complete sentences, proper English, and a polite approach are appropriate. When the subscription information says *listserv,* assume that you are talking to a machine and use the commands described earlier in the chapter.

You'll generally get a welcome message when you subscribe to a list. This message tells you the purpose of the list and other useful information. Sometimes a list is aimed at particular countries or regions. While these lists are not focused on genealogy, the list owners have indicated that genealogy is an acceptable, although in some cases unusual, subject for the list.

The mailing lists included here address many subjects, some only tangentially touching genealogy. Some touch on heritage, culture, and the genealogy of particular ethnic groups. Some concentrate on specific family names, some on specific historical periods. Some address software and computer-related topics that may be of interest to online genealogists. The list here will get you started. Be on the lookout for messages that contain the names of other lists. But be careful how many lists you sign up for: things could snowball if you belong to just three very active groups. Just remember to come up for air once in a while!

General Genealogy Lists

These are lists about general genealogy, apart from any specific ethnic group, surname, region, or historical period. Beginners should explore these first.

- *Adoptees.* This list is a place for adoptees to share information, experiences, and feelings as related to adoption search, reunion, and many other adoption-related issues. Membership is restricted to adoptees and *adoptee-lites*, who are people who were raised without one or both birth parents but who were never legally adopted. This list has an associated Web site, the Adoptees Internet Mailing List Web site at http://www.webreflection.com/aiml/ (see Fig. 4-7). To subscribe, send e-mail to listserv@maelstrom.stjohns.edu with the following message: SUBSCRIBE ADOPTEES firstname lastname. The address for posting is adoptees@maelstrom.stjohns.edu.

- *Adoption.* Discussions of anything and everything connected with adoption. To subscribe, send e-mail to adoption-request@listserv.law .cornell.edu with the message SUBSCRIBE ADOPTION firstname lastname. The address for posting is adoption@listserv.law.cornell.edu.

- *BrthPrnt.* Mailing list open to anyone wanting to discuss birth-family issues. To subscribe, send e-mail to listserv@indycms.iupui.edu with the message SUB BRTHPRNT firstname lastname. The address for posting is bras-net-request@cs.columbia.edu.

Figure 4-7
The Adoptees Internet Mailing List is one of many mailing lists with an associated Web site.

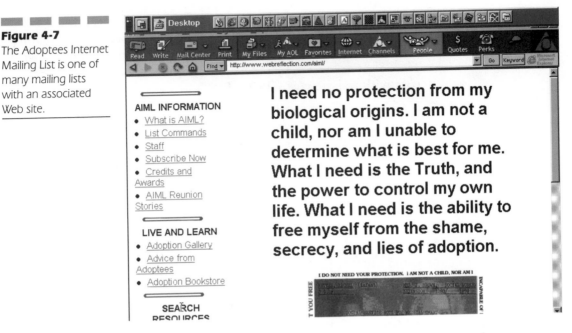

- *Elijah-L.* A list for believing members of the Church of Jesus Christ of Latter-Day Saints to discuss their ideas and experiences relating to genealogy in the LDS Church. There's not much data in this list but more of discussion about technique and methodology, especially as it affects their theology. You can join even if you're not Mormon, as long as you don't deliberately insult their beliefs. To subscribe, send e-mail to Elijah-L-Request@genealogy.emcee.com with the subject ARCHIVE and the message GET CHARTER. After reading and agreeing to the charter, you can follow the instructions above to subscribe.

- *GenMsc.* This group's messages also appear in the soc.genealogy.misc newsgroup. It covers general genealogical discussions that aren't specific enough for one of the other soc.genealogy.* newsgroups. To post, send messages to genmsc-l@rootsweb.com. To subscribe send a message that says only "subscribe" (without the quotes) to genmsc-l-request@rootsweb.com (mail mode), genmsc-d-request@rootsweb.com (digest mode), or genmsc-i-request@rootsweb.com (index mode).

- *GenMtd.* This group's messages also appear in soc.genealogy.methods newsgroup. It discusses general genealogy research techniques and resources. To post a message, send it to genmtd-l@rootsweb.com. Send a message that says only *subscribe* in the text to genmtd-l-request@rootsweb.com (mail mode), genmtd-d-request@rootsweb.com (digest mode), or genmtd-i-request@rootsweb.com (index mode).

- *Gen-Newbie-L.*   A message exchange mailing list for the beginner, where the most basic genealogy questions are answered. This mailing list has an associated Web page at http://www.rootsweb.com/~newbie/ (Fig. 4-8). To subscribe, send e-mail to gen-newbie-l-request@rootsweb .com with the message SUBSCRIBE.

- *ROOTS-L.*   This is probably the best-known genealogy mailing list in the world, with thousands of subscribers. We discussed ROOTS-L in detail earlier in this chapter. To subscribe, send e-mail to roots-l-request@rootsweb.com with the message SUBSCRIBE.

Ethnic Groups

These lists aren't specifically about genealogy but cover the culture, history, and current events of particular ethnic groups. Most of them will accept the occasional genealogy query, and they're great places to lurk if you want to learn a little bit about other people.

- *AfriGeneas.*   A private mailing list created as a place to discuss and promote family history research. This is a place to look for African

Figure 4-8

If you are new to genealogy, or new to computers, this is a great Web site to visit.

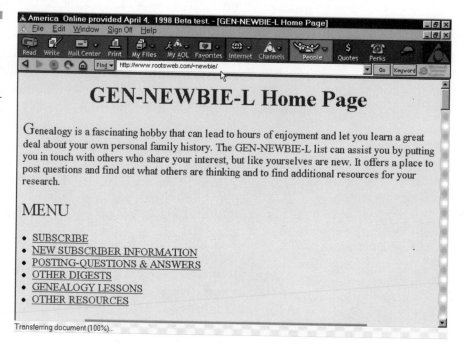

ancestors as well as to discuss genealogical interests, history, culture, and resources. Discussion areas include, but are not limited to, queries on surnames, records/events, how do I start, census, locations, people and places, and resources. Messages about research, queries, and resources go to afrigeneas@msstate.edu. Request to be added to the list by sending a message to afrigeneas-request@msstate.edu.

- *AfroAm-L.*   A discussion group focusing on issues concerning African-Americans in everyday life. This is an extremely busy list, with rates of 25 messages an hour possible. While you may not want to post specific genealogy queries, you could send messages that address broader areas of interest to genealogists: migration routes, historical events and documents, surname origins, and so forth. To subscribe, send e-mail to listserv@harvarda.harvard.edu with the following message: SUBSCRIBE AFROAM-L firstname lastname. The mailing address for postings is afroam-l@harvarda.harvard.edu.

- *Albanian.*   A mailing list dedicated to the exchange of news and discussion of issues on Albania, the Albanian people living in Albania and other areas of the Balkans (Kosova, Macedonia, Montenegro), and Albanians living elsewhere in the world. The news and discussion are conducted in Albanian and English. To subscribe, send e-mail to listserv@ubvm.cc.buffalo.edu with a message of SUBSCRIBE ALBANIAN firstname lastname. The mailing address for postings is albanian@ubvm.cc.buffalo.edu.

- *APSA-L.*   A list devoted to the subject of literature and cultures of the Portuguese-speaking world, especially Brazil and Portugal. Although associated with the American Portuguese Studies Association (APSA), the list is not restricted to members of the association. To subscribe, send e-mail to majordomo@beacon.bryant.edu with the message SUBSCRIBE APSA-L. The mailing address for postings is also majordomo@beacon.bryant.edu.

- *Argentina.*   General discussion and information on Argentina and Latin American social or political issues. The messages in this list are almost exclusively in Spanish. To subscribe, send your name, e-mail address, phone number, postal mail address, and topics of interest to argentina-requests@journal.math.indiana.edu. The address for postings is argentina@journal.math.indiana.edu. Note that this is the main list; there are several sublists concerning more specialized aspects of Argentina.

- *Balt-L.*   Devoted to communications with, and discussions about, the Baltic Republics of Lithuania, Latvia, and Estonia. Subscription to this list is open to anyone with skills or interests relevant to the Baltics, or to anyone who just wants to know what's going on. Short requests to help locate families or villages are carried in general-interest digest messages. To subscribe, send e-mail to listserv@listserv.acsu.buffalo.edu with the message SUB BALT-L firstname lastname. The address for postings is balt-l@ubvm.cc.buffalo.edu.

- *Banat.*   A mailing list for people doing research into the Banat region of what was formerly Hungary, Romania, and Yugoslavia. To subscribe, send e-mail to banat-l-request@rootsweb.com with the message SUBSCRIBE.

- *Basque-L.*   This list is a forum for the exchange and dissemination of information on Basque culture. Genealogy-related issues are often discussed on the list, though the main topics of discussion are social and political current affairs, gastronomy, Basque music, poetry, anthropology (specifically the origin of the Basques), and similar subjects. Basque, Spanish, French, and English are used on the list, and other languages are welcome. To subscribe, send e-mail to listserve@cunyvm .cuny.edu with the message SUBSCRIBE BASQUE-L. The address for posting is basque-l@cunyvm.cuny.edu.

- *Brazil.*   A RootsWeb mailing list concerning genealogy in Brazil; most of the messages are in Portuguese. The mailing address for postings is brazil-l@rootsweb.com. To subscribe send the word "subscribe" (without quotes) as the only text in the body of a message to brazil-l-request@rootsweb.com (mail mode) or brazil-d-request@rootsweb.com (digest mode).

- *Canadian-Roots-L.*   The Canadian version of Roots-L. To subscribe send SUB CANADIAN-ROOTS-L firstname lastname to listserv@listserv .indiana.edu. After you have joined, you send postings to canadian-roots-l@listserv.indiana.edu.

- *Catrachos.*   Topics related to the Honduras, not exclusively genealogy. The languages of preference are English and Spanish. The topics of discussion range from local interest to politics. To subscribe, send a politely worded request to stanmarder@aol.com (Stanley Marder). The address for posting is catrachos@andrew.cmu.edu.

- *CentAm-L.*   You'll find students from Central America and people interested in discussing issues concerning Guatemala, Belize, Honduras, El Salvador, Nicaragua, Costa Rica, and Panama here. The focus is not strictly genealogy. To subscribe, send e-mail to listserv@ubvm .cc.buffalo.edu with the message SUBSCRIBE CENTAM-L firstname lastname. The address for posting is centam-l@ubvm.cc.buffalo.edu.

- *Ec-Charla.*   The messages on this list are mainly in Spanish and discuss issues concerning Ecuador, not strictly genealogy. To subscribe, send e-mail to listproc@lac.net with the following message: SUBSCRIBE EC-CHARLA firstname lastname.

- *Gen-DE-L.*   Gatewayed in the soc.genealogy.german newsgroup for the discussion of German genealogy, you subscribe by sending e-mail to gen-de-l-request@rootsweb.com with the text *subscribe*. The address for posting is gen-de-l@rootsweb.com.

- *Gen-FR-L.*   Messages from the fr.rec.genealogie newsgroup are mirrored here. It discusses, in French, the genealogy of French-speaking people. To subscribe send "subscribe" (without the quotes) as the only text in the body of a message to gen-fr-l-request@rootsweb.com (mail mode), gen-fr-d-request@rootsweb.com (digest mode), or gen-fr-i-request@rootsweb.com (index mode). The posting address is gen-fr-l@rootsweb.com.

- *Poland-Roots.*   Discussion of Polish genealogy data and methods. You can't post until you subscribe; the owner will send you instructions for posting. To subscribe, send a message that says only "subscribe" (no quotes) to poland-roots-request@rootsweb.com (mail mode) or poland-roots-d-request@rootsweb.com (digest mode).

- *Ger-Rus.*   Germans from Russia discuss culture and folklore here. To subscribe, send e-mail to listserv@listserv.nodak.edu with the following message: SUBSCRIBE GER-RUS firstname lastname. The address for posting is ger-rus@listserv.nodak.edu.

- *Hungary.*   Topics related to Hungary and the Austrian Empire genealogy and history. You can't post until you subscribe. Send a message with only the word "subscribe" (no quotes) in the body to hungary-l-request@rootsweb.com (mail mode) or hungary-d-request@rootsweb.com (digest mode).

- *Indian-Roots-L.*   Discussions of Native American genealogical and historical research. To subscribe, send e-mail to listserv@listserv.indiana.edu with the message SUB INDIAN-ROOTS-L firstname lastname.

- *JewishGen.*   Discussions of Jewish genealogy. Mirrored with the soc.genealogy.jewish newsgroup. (JEWGEN is a synonym for JEWISHGEN and postings to both will just give subscribers two copies of the same message.) To subscribe, send e-mail to listserv@apple.ease.lsoft.com with the message SUBSCRIBE JEWISHGEN firstname lastname.

- *Llajta.*   Bolivia, in all aspects, in Spanish, English, Quechua, and Portuguese. To subscribe, send e-mail to listserv@io.dsd.litton.com with the message SUBSCRIBE LLAJTA firstname lastname. The address for posting is llajta@io.dsd.litton.com.

■ *Makedon.*   The Macedonian Republic is discussed in this moderated list; it is not strictly about genealogy. The postings are mirrored to INFORMA—BBS in Macedonia. Messages are mainly in Macedonian, with some English messages. To subscribe, send e-mail to listserv@ubvm.cc.buffalo.edu with the following message: SUBSCRIBE MAKEDON firstname lastname. The address for posting is makedon@ubvm.cc.buffalo.edu.

■ *NamNet.*   Anything related to Namibia. Small postings preferred. To subscribe, send e-mail to namnet-request@lisse.na with the message SUBSCRIBE. The address for posting is namnet@lisse.na.

■ *Peru.*   Peru's history, current events, culture, and so forth are discussed; it is not strictly genealogical. Unlike many lists, this one is an echo site. All messages just get bounced from this address to the people subscribed. To subscribe, send e-mail to listproc@cs.sfsu.edu with the message SUBSCRIBE PERU firstname lastname. The Subject line of this message must be empty. The address for posting is peru@cs.sfsu.edu.

■ *Pie.*   Pie stands for Pursuing (Our Italian Names Together) In E-mail. This list discusses Italian genealogy as does its companion Web site (http://www.cimorelli.com/pie/piehome.htm). The easiest way to subscribe is to go to http://www.cimorelli.com/pie/cfopie/subpie.htm and fill out the form.

■ *Russian-Jews.*   This list discusses history, announces upcoming events, and shares information; genealogy isn't the focus but is accepted. To subscribe, send e-mail to listproc@shamash.org with the message SUB RUSSIAN-JEWS firstname lastname. The address for posting is russian-jews@shamash.org.

■ *Slovak-L.*   A list for anyone interested in Slovak history, culture, politics, social life, economy, and anything else concerning the Republic of Slovakia and its people or their descendants in other countries. The list is unmoderated and unlimited in scope. To subscribe, send e-mail to listserv@ubvm.cc.buffalo.edu with the message SUBSCRIBE SLOVAK-L firstname lastname. The address for posting is slovak-world@ubvm.cc.buffalo.edu.

■ *Slovak-World.*   An unmoderated list that can be used to contact Slovaks around the world. The goal is to help people find lost contacts, join relatives, meet new friends, and so on. It is not limited as to territory or language and is open to all who have something in common with Slovaks and Slovakia. To subscribe, send e-mail to listproc@fris.sk with the message SUBSCRIBE SLOVAK-WORLD firstname lastname. The address for posting is slovak-world@fris.sk.

- *Sudan-L.*   A forum for sharing experience, ideas, thoughts, comments, and sources of information on issues concerning Sudan. To subscribe, send e-mail to listserv@emuvml.cc.emory.edu with the message SUBSCRIBE SUDAN-L firstname lastname. The address for posting is sudan-l@emuvml.cc.emory.edu (you must be a subscriber to post to this list).

- *Welsh-L.*   Discussion of Welsh language, Welsh culture, history, and politics, and to offer a forum for speakers and students of the Welsh language; however, this list will accept genealogical queries in Welsh. English may be used on WELSH-L to discuss questions of grammar, not questions of Grandma! To subscribe, send e-mail to listserv@irlearn.ucd.ie with the following message: SUBSCRIBE WELSH-L firstname lastname. The address for posting is welsh-l@irlearn.ucd.ie.

Family Name Lists

These lists are for specific surnames or families. You usually have to request permission to join one of these lists. There are now too many to list! You can go to AOL's Keyword: *Mailing List* and click **Browse the Directory**. This will take you to the Web site http://www.idot.aol.com/mld/production/, where you can click on the word **search** and enter in the term box the surnames you want. Click on the **search** button and see what happens!

I also suggest you check out these sites to search for mailing lists that cover the surnames you are interested in.

Genealogy Resources on the Internet: Surnames (http://members.aol.com/gresinet/gen_mail_surnames-gen.html).   This page is a list of general surname search/query mailing lists. Some are regional (such as SURNAMES-IRELAND). Others are very general, such as the Roots Surname List. Instructions for subscribing are included in each list.

Genealogy Resources on the Internet: Mailing Lists (http://members.aol.com/johnfl4246/gen_mail.html).   Scroll down this page to the fifth entry. Click on a letter of the alphabet and search for your surnames.

The Internet Sleuth: Surnames (http://isleuth.com/surnames.html).   This is a Web-Search catalog, with a genealogy category and a surnames subcategory. You'll find not only mailing lists but also other Internet resources (databases, Web pages, etc.) here.

Genealogy Listservers, Newsgroups, and Special Home Pages (http://www.eskimo .com/~chance/lists.html).   This is a searchable list of resources on surnames and localities. You can either click on a letter for an alphabetized table of contents or enter a name in the search box. It's not as complete as the Genealogy Resources on the Internet pages, but it seems to be updated often.

Historical Groups

These lists focus on historical events or groups that could be invaluable to you in your genealogy research.

- *Civil-War.*   The American Civil War, history and issues including genealogy. Subscribe by sending the word *subscribe* as a message to civil-war-request@rootsweb.com (mail mode) or civil-war-d-request@rootsweb.com (digest mode). Post messages to civil-war@rootsweb.com.

- *Gen-Medieval-L.*   These messages also appear in soc.genealogy .medieval for genealogy and family history discussions among people researching individuals living during medieval times. Medieval times are loosely defined as the period from the breakup of the Western Roman Empire until the time public records relating to the general population began to be kept and extending roughly from A.D. 500 to A.D. 1600. To subscribe, send an e-mail message with *subscribe* to gen-medieval-l-request@rootsweb.com (mail mode), gen-medieval-d-request@rootsweb.com (digest mode), or gen-medieval-i-request@rootsweb.com (index mode). Post messages to gen-medieval-l@rootsweb.com.

- *Mayflower.*   All Mayflower descendents, any time, any place. Mailing address for postings is mayflower-l@rootsweb.com. To subscribe send the word "subscribe" (without the quotes) as the only text in the body of a message to mayflower-l-request@rootsweb.com (mail mode) or mayflower-d-request@rootsweb.com (digest mode).

- *RusHist.*   All aspects of Russian history from the reign of Ivan III (1462–1505) to the end of the Romanov dynasty in the person of Nicholas II (1894–1917), including but not limited to genealogy. To subscribe, send e-mail to listserv@vm.usc.edu with the message SUBSCRIBE RUSHIST firstname lastname. The address for posting is rushist@vm.usc.edu.

- *Overland-Trails.*   This list is limited to discussions concerning the history, preservation, and promotion of the Oregon, California, Santa Fe, and other historic trails in the Western United States. To subscribe, send e-mail to listserv@calcite.rocky.edu with the following message: SUBSCRIBE OVERLAND-TRAILS firstname lastname. The address for posting is overland-trails@calcite.rocky.edu. You must be subscribed to post messages.

Regional Groups

These mailing lists focus on specific geographic areas.

- *Western-Roots-L.*   Discussions of genealogical and historical research in Washington, Oregon, Alaska, Idaho, Montana, Wyoming, California, Nevada, Hawaii, Colorado, Utah, Arizona, and New Mexico. You subscribe with the message SUB WESTERN_ROOTS_L firstname lastname to listserv@listserv.indiana.edu. Once you are subscribed, you are allowed to post messages to western-roots-l@listserv.indiana.edu.

- *Deep-South-Roots.*   A genealogy discussion list for the Mississippi-Alabama-Georgia-Florida region. To subscribe, send e-mail to deep-south-roots-l@listserv.indiana.edu with the following message: SUB DEEP-SOUTH-ROOTS-L firstname lastname. Messages go to deep-south-roots-l@listserv.indiana.edu.

- *Maggie_Ohio.*   This list is designed to provide a discussion forum for anyone who has an interest in genealogy in the state of Ohio. Send the word *subscribe* as the only text in a message to Maggie_Ohio-D-request@rootsweb.com.

- *Far-West-Roots.*   A genealogy discussion list for the California-Nevada-Hawaii region. To subscribe, send e-mail to maiser@rmgate.pop.indiana.edu with the message SUB FAR-WEST-ROOTS.

- *KYRoots.*   Discussions of Kentucky genealogy and historical research. To subscribe, send e-mail to listserv@lsv.uky.edu with the message SUBSCRIBE KYROOTS firstname lastname.

- *VA-Roots.*   A discussion list for Virginia genealogy. To subscribe, send e-mail to listserver@leo.vsla.edu with the following message: subscribe VA-ROOTS firstname lastname.

Software Lists

These lists have information about genealogical software and computer standards (like GEDCOM) of interest to genealogists.

- *GenCmp-L.*   A general discussion of genealogy and its relation to computers and computing. To subscribe, send e-mail to listserv@apple .ease.lsoft.com with the message SUB GENCMP-L firstname lastname. *Note:* This list usually subscribes you in digest mode. If you want mail mode, you must send a second message to the list server: SET GENCMP-L MAIL.

- *BK-L.*   A place to exchange experiences related to the Brother's Keeper program. To subscribe, send e-mail to bk5-l-request@genealogy .emcee.com with the subject "subscribe" (no quotes) and no message body. The address for posting is bk5-l@-genealogy.emcee.com.

- *Family-Origins-Users.*   If you use the Family Origins genealogy software program, this list is to interact with other users, seek help in using the program, and exchange ideas and solutions regarding problem areas. To subscribe, send the word "subscribe" (without the quotes) as the only text in the body of a message to family-origins-users-l-request@rootsweb.com (mail mode) or family-origins-users-d-request@rootsweb.com (digest mode). Post messages to family-origins-users-l@rootsweb.com.

- *GEDCOM-L.*   A technical mailing list to discuss the GEDCOM specifications. If you aren't a computer programmer, a serious genealogical computer user, or haven't read the GEDCOM specification, this list is definitely not for you. To subscribe, send e-mail to listserv@vm1 .nodak.edu with the message SUB GEDCOM-L firstname lastname. The address for posting is gedcom-l@vm1.nodak.edu.

- *PAF.*   Mailing list for discussion of issues relating to the Personal Ancestral File genealogy program. To subscribe, send e-mail to majordomo@rehtori.kasanen.fi with the message SUBSCRIBE PAF. The address for posting is paf@rehtori.kasanen.fi.

- *GenWeb.*   A discussion list for ROOTSBOOK, a project to link genealogy trees on a mass basis. To subscribe, send e-mail to listserv@ucsd .edu with the message SUB GENWEB.

E-mail Newsletters

Another e-mail resource is the newsletter. Unlike interactive mailing lists, newsletters are meant to be read like a magazine. You can write letters to the editor if you like, but you won't often see them in the newsletters. Two e-mail newsletters are worthy of note.

- *Eastman's Genealogy Index* (http://www.ancestry.com/home/times.htm). This is a weekly all-text newsletter on genealogy topics. A typical issue will cover reviews of genealogy computer programs; news items of note to genealogists; a list of Web sites to visit; book, CD-ROM, and TV reviews; and more. The reviews in this newsletter are specific, without being verbose, and honest. Each issue is posted at the site listed above, as well as e-mailed to subscribers. You can also find back issues here. To subscribe, send e-mail to subscribe@rootscomputing .com with the subject: SUBSCRIBE.

- *Treasure Maps Newsletter* (http://www.firstct.com/fv/sub.html). Treasure Maps (Fig. 4-9) is one of the best sites on the Web for novices. It is aimed at hands-on, how-to information to help you actually do research online. To keep track of the latest news on Treasure Maps, you might want to subscribe to their monthly newsletter. The

Figure 4-9

The Treasure Maps site is a great tool for learning how to know more about our ancestors.

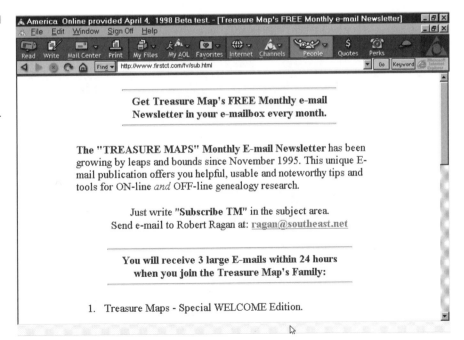

Figure 4-10
Rootsweb hosts hundreds of genealogy-related mailing lists.

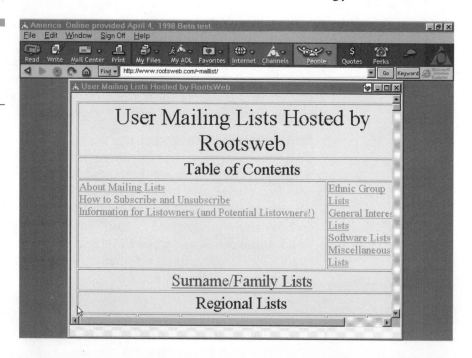

Figure 4-11
The AOL Mail Center can be a starting point in your genealogy searches.

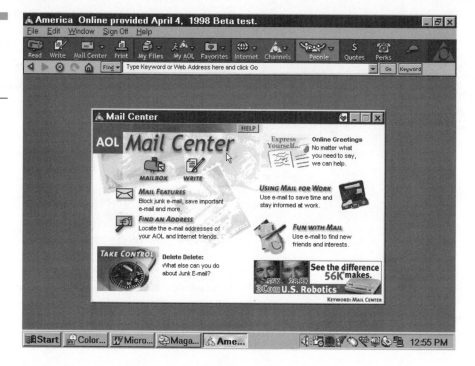

newsletter also has genealogy information that hasn't been released yet. To subscribe, send an e-mail message to ragan@southeast.net with the subject: SUBSCRIBE TM. Within 24 hours, you should receive your first issue as well as a help file telling you how to make the program work best.

■ *Genealogy Today Newsletter.*   Note the home page at http://www.enoch .com/genealogy/newslet.htm. This monthly newsletter has tips, information, meetings and seminar announcements, and queries. To subscribe, just send e-mail to GenToday-L-request@rootsweb.com and type only the word subscribe. You may also submit a query by e-mailing it to tfarris268@aol.com with Query in the subject line.

Finding More Mailing Lists

While we've provided dozens of mailing lists for you to start your online genealogy research, you may want more. Don't forget AOL's Keyword: *MAILING LISTS,* where you can search and browse for topics. In addition, the folks at the Rootsweb World Wide Web site have many mailing lists and are adding more each week. Use AOL's browser to go to http://www .rootsweb.com/~maillist/; you'll have access to the hundreds of mailing lists hosted by Rootsweb. Figure 4-10 shows the table of contents for this genealogy mailing list treasure trove. Figure 4-11 shows you the AOL Mailing List search window.

CHAPTER 5

Newsgroups

Internet newsgroups can be a confusing subject. To begin with, Internet newsgroups don't really reside on the Internet; they're actually on Usenet, which is a parallel network that is interconnected with the Internet. For simplicity, we'll refer to Usenet newsgroups as just newsgroups.

Newsgroups are similar in many ways to mailing lists. Newsgroups are electronic discussion groups where subscribers can send and receive messages. Messages sent to the newsgroup can be read by anyone who subscribes to the newsgroup. Many newsgroups of interest to genealogists are available on the Internet. Newsgroups can be moderated or unmoderated.

But there are differences between newsgroups and mailing lists. Mailing lists deliver messages to your electronic mailbox automatically, and you can use any e-mail program to participate in a mailing list. You need a special program to participate in newsgroups, and the messages don't come to you—you have to actively go get them.

Another big difference between mailing lists and newsgroups is that you may not have access to every newsgroup you are interested in, whether or not you are eligible to join. That's because your Internet Service Provider (in this case America Online) has to choose which newsgroups it will carry.

You might wonder why America Online wouldn't just carry every newsgroup there is. The answer is simple—there are too many newsgroups, carrying too many messages, many of which aren't appropriate for a family service like AOL. Leaving aside the issue of adult content on newsgroups (much of the ruckus about pornography on the Internet is triggered by the content of certain newsgroups), there is just too much material flowing through newsgroups.

No one can say exactly how much material flows through newsgroups in a day, but the amount is staggering. Consider that there are more than 50,000 newsgroups, with more than 900,000 new messages posted every day!

So, while AOL doesn't carry every newsgroup in existence, the built-in newsreader program makes it easy to participate in the newsgroups that are carried. And AOL does carry thousands of newsgroups, including many that are of direct or indirect interest to genealogists.

A Little Background

To enjoy Usenet, you need to know something about the culture and history of this Internet service. Usenet is about 20 years old, and grew from an academic message system to a worldwide exchange of files and communication. Today, there are tens of thousands of newsgroups (including numerous genealogy-related ones) and commercial connections included in Usenet. In fact, there are more business connections than educational.

Most Usenet newsgroups are open, free (perhaps chaotic!), and not at all edited or moderated. Some, however, are moderated, and the moderator can ask you to leave the group if you are disruptive. More about that later.

Although many people are connected through and because of their jobs, most newsgroups should not be used for advertising. Commercials are tolerated only when they're infrequent, informative, low-key, and preferably in direct response to a specific question. The only exception is the .biz groups, where advertisements are accepted.

Newsgroups are not strictly an American phenomenon. Many, many users are from other countries, often speaking English as a second language, so be tolerant about grammar and spelling.

No person or group has control over all the newsgroups. No person or group authorizes who gets access to newsgroups, which articles are propagated where, who can post articles, or anything else. These things are handled one newsgroup at a time. This means that, although the freedoms of expression and association are almost absolute, Usenet is not a democracy. It's anarchy, with little control except as exerted by the social pressures of those participating.

A *moderated* newsgroup has a referee (a person who decides what messages get to go on that newsgroup). An *unmoderated* newsgroup isn't edited in any way, except you'll likely get flamed (insulted) if you post a message off the proper topic. Most newsgroups are unmoderated.

There are eight major categories of newsgroups:

- ALT for alternative topics, or for those that just don't fit exactly elsewhere
- BIZ for commercial activity
- COMP for computer science—related topics
- MISC for miscellaneous items
- NEWS for topics about Usenet itself
- REC for recreation
- SCI for science not related to computers
- SOC for social interaction and hobbies (Most genealogy newsgroups are in this category.)
- TALK for general conversation, usually to no purpose at all

Most of the genealogy newsgroups are in the .soc area, as you'll see in the section "Newsgroups of Interest to Online Genealogists." But before you put newsgroups to work in your genealogical research, there are a few other topics you have to cover—the next one up is etiquette.

Internet Etiquette and Tips on Newsgroups

Etiquette may not seem like a likely topic for a computer book, but it really is. If you think of the group of people who participate in a newsgroup as a community, then you are halfway there. Just like any other community, newsgroups have their own etiquette, or way people are expected to behave when they are in the community. The forms of etiquette practiced in newsgroups are variants on the more general etiquette of the Internet as a whole, commonly referred to as *netiquette*.

NOTE   *Many of the same etiquette issues apply to mailing lists as well. But newsgroups have a well-deserved reputation for being less well-mannered than most of us would like. Some people just can't understand why the rest of us aren't interested in their get-rich-quick schemes, their porno sites, or the number of ways they can insult someone else. The presence of rude people in newsgroups makes practicing proper netiquette even more important.*

Here are the basic rules you should observe when working with newsgroups, or the Net in general.

- Rule Number One: Stay on topic, or you might receive more *flames* (insulting, angry messages) than useful responses. In general, these topics are welcomed in the genealogy newsgroups:

  Almost any message about genealogy in general.

  Announcements and information on upcoming genealogical meetings, workshops, symposiums, reunions, and so on.

  Reviews, criticisms, and comments regarding software or hardware you've used about genealogy/family history.

  Telling others about bookshops and online vendors around the world that sell books or information about this subject.

Your own family history information and requests for others to help you find information. Tiny tafels (ASCII files of the names and locations you are searching in a defined format; see Appendix B) are often posted for this.

- It is okay to go off on a tangent occasionally, and indeed such discussions can be very educational, if they add to everybody's understanding and enjoyment of genealogy. But remember Rule Number One!

- Courtesy (and rudeness!) can be catching. Spread the good stuff.

- Don't think you can hide behind the modem. Remember that your postings and comments might be seen by tens of thousands of people in many different countries throughout the world, and you may run into some of them in person.

- Carefully read what you receive to be certain that you understand the message before you reply.

- Carefully read what you send, to ensure your message won't be misunderstood. Don't be too quick to click that **Send** button: let a reply sit overnight if it might be provocative, then read it again before sending. This prevents that sinking feeling of regret when you realize what you posted is not what you meant. What you send is posted as you sent it, unless you send it to a moderated group, where all messages must pass the moderator's muster.

- Avoid sarcasm. If humor seems appropriate, clearly label it as such. A smiley face such as this ;-) should indicate humor. It's easy to misunderstand what's being said when there's no tone of voice, facial expressions, or body language to go by.

- Double-check addresses. Try not to post to the wrong newsgroups by mistake.

- Be tolerant of newcomers, as you expect others to be tolerant of you. None of us were born knowing all about computers, genealogy, or the Internet. Don't abuse new users for their lack of knowledge. As you become more expert, be patient as others first learn to paddle, then swim, then surf the Net. Be an active participant in teaching them.

- Avoid cluttering your messages with excessive emphasis (**, !!, >>, and so on). It can make the message hard to follow.

- When you respond to a message, either include the relevant part of the original message or explicitly refer to the original's contents. Often people sort Usenet so that the most recent articles come first; therefore they will see the reply before they see the original message. (Remember the convention of preceding each quoted line of the original message you include with the > character.) However, never quote more than necessary to make your point clear, and don't quote the entire message. In America Online's newsreader, the original message is to your left. You highlight the pertinent part and click the "Quote" button to include it in your reply.

- Good subject lines mean your message will be read. The point of the subject line is to get the attention of people who should read the message, and the only way to do that is to make sure the subject line describes the main point of your message. More about that in a moment.

- Keep messages to only one subject. This allows readers to quickly decide whether they need to read the message in full. Second subjects within a single message are often missed. Questions are often the exception to this rule. If you're seeking information about a family, include the surname in uppercase in the message subject. Many readers don't have time to read the contents of all messages. The topic of subject lines is discussed in more detail later in this section.

- All questions concerning the possibility of access to the LDS database from the Internet will be answered "no," so please don't ask. No one has electronic access to the LDS (Latter-Day Saints) database. Period. Please see Chapter 9 for more information.

- Be specific, especially when asking questions. If you ask about a person, identify when and where the person might have lived. In questions concerning specific genealogical software, make it clear what sort of computer (PC/MS-DOS, PC/Windows, Apple Macintosh, etc.) is involved. The folks reading these newsgroups are very helpful but very busy, and are more likely to answer if they don't have to ask what you mean.

- Always, always put your name in the text of your message, and your best e-mail address for a reply. The end of the message is a good place for your name and e-mail address. However, some people avoid putting their exact reply address so that they don't get unsolicited junk email. The way to do this: "Reply to: libbic AT aol.com"

- Whenever any newsgroup posts a FAQ, **read it**. If you can't find a FAQ message or file, make one of your first questions on the group, "Where and when can I get the Frequently Asked Questions for this group?"

- On certain days holidays, snowstorms, or other events keep people home from work, so the Usenet newsgroups have unusually high traffic because so many people found themselves unable to, or not required to, go to work. In that case, you must choose what to read based on subject line or sender, because it's impossible to read everything posted to the group that day.

Good and Bad Subject Lines

Since creating effective subject lines is so important, here are some examples of good and bad subject lines to guide you:

Bad: *Wondering if anyone is looking for JONES*

Good: *Researching surname JONES*

Good: *SPENCER: England>MA>NY>OH>IN>MS*

Good: *SC POWELLs, pre-1845*

Good: *? Civil War Records*

In the good examples, note these conventions: Surnames are in all caps, but nothing else. Although text in all uppercase is generally considered shouting, the exception to this rule in the case of genealogy newsgroups is that surnames should be in uppercase, just as in any query. An arrow (>) is used to denote migration from one place to another. A date is always helpful. If your message is a question, indicate that in the subject line.

Notice that a question message will have a subject line that starts with a question mark. In the body of the message, when you ask a question, end it with a question mark and press the **Return** key. That should be the end of that line. This makes it much easier for people to reply, because most newsreaders will quote the original message line by line.

Newsgroups and America Online

America Online includes a newsreader in its software. This section walks you through the entire process of finding a newsgroup, subscribing, reading a message, composing a reply, and unsubscribing from the newsgroup. Get ready.

You can call up the America Online Usenet window in several ways. In the drop-down **Internet** menu you can choose Usenet. The Keyword for newsgroups is USENET. Type that into the Address box, or press **CTRL-K** (or click the **Keyword** button on the tool bar) and type it in the dialog box. You can update your shortcuts, too, by clicking Favorites, My Shortcuts, Edit and adding USENET to the list.

NOTE   *The first time you use the Newsgroups keyword, AOL offers you the option to filter out junk posts. Junk posts are the newsgroup equivalent of the junk mail that floods all of our real-world mailboxes. You can toggle the junk posts filter on and off by clicking Preferences in the Usenet window, and adding or removing the check mark.*

Finding and Subscribing to Newsgroups

However you get there, once you reach the Newsgroups window, you'll see something like Fig. 5-1. There are all sorts of options and settings you can play with here, and you should explore them—later. For now, the goal is to learn enough to start doing some genealogical research.

The easiest way to find a newsgroup you want to read is to click the **Search All Newsgroups** button. This lets you enter all or part of the newsgroup name you're interested in. Say you choose the word *genealogy.* Type it in and click **Search**. In a moment or two AOL will display a list of all the newsgroups with the word genealogy in their title. In early 1998, America Online carried 37 newsgroups with the word genealogy in their titles.

When you see the list of newsgroups that match your search, double click the listing to view the description. The window will have a link to subscribe, a link to look at current articles, and a brief description. If you decide you want to subscribe to that newsgroup, click **Susbcribe to newsgroup....** This adds the newsgroup to your personal list.

What if you know the name of the newsgroup you want to subscribe to, but when you enter that name in AOL's Search Newsgroups window, the newsgroup doesn't show up? Don't give up, try Expert Add first. In the main Newsgroups window, click the **Expert Add** button. In the Expert Add window that appears, type the full name of the newsgroup, then click **Add**. If AOL can give you access to that newsgroup, it will be added to your personal list.

Figure 5-1
The main Newsgroups
window.

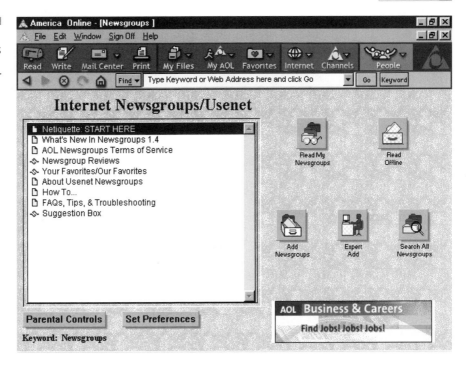

Managing Newsgroups and Reading or Sending Messages

To see the list of newsgroups you are subscribed to, go to the main News-groups window, and click **Read My Newsgroups**. You'll see the Read My Newsgroups window, which will look a lot like the one in Fig. 5-2.

As you might expect, you select a particular newsgroup by clicking on it, then tell AOL what you want to do with that newsgroup by clicking one of the buttons at the top or bottom of the window. The following list tells you what each of the buttons in Fig. 5-2 does:

- *Internet Names.* The newsgroups shown in the Show My Newsgroups window are all listed by Internet name. Click this button to see a short English-language name and description for each newsgroup in your personal list.

- *Mark All Newsgroups Read.* Messages can often come in faster than you can deal with them. With this button, you can say, "The heck with it, I can't read all these messages." Click it, and you'll tell AOL to

Figure 5-2
A typical view of the
Read My Newsgroups
window.

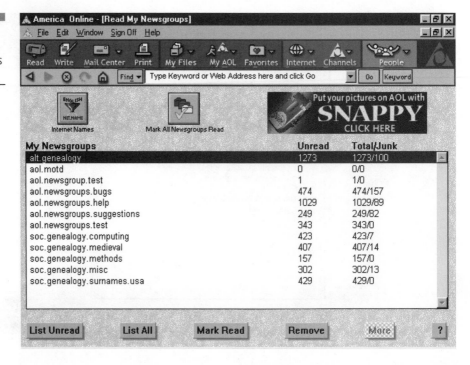

treat all the messages in all the newsgroups you are currently subscribed to as if they had already been read. Instead of hundreds or
thousands of unread messages, you'll have none (at least for a few
minutes).

■ *List Unread.*   This button tells the newsreader program to display all
the unread messages in the currently selected newsgroup.

■ *List All.*   This button causes the newsreader program to display every
message available for the selected newsgroup, whether or not you've
already read those messages.

■ *Mark Read.*   This button tells AOL to mark all the messages in the
selected newsgroup as read.

■ *Remove.*   This button deletes the selected newsgroup from the list.
Note that this doesn't affect the original newsgroup in any way, it just
removes the references to that link.

■ *More.*   If you subscribe to enough newsgroups, the **More** button will
appear. Click this button to see the parts of a list that aren't already
visible on the Web site.

When you are ready to read the messages in one of your newsgroups, click **List All** or **List Unread**. In most cases, you want to use **List Unread**, as there is little point in having to sort through all the messages you've read recently to find the ones you haven't.

━━ ━━ ━━ ━━ ━━ ━━ ━━ ━━ ━━ ━━ ━━ ━━ ━━ ━━ ━━

NOTE *AOL doesn't keep a permanent list of all the messages you have or haven't read. All messages referred to in this section, whether read or unread, are messages that AOL happens to have for a particular newsgroup right now. As new messages are added to the group, old ones get pushed out. A consequence of this is that you may miss messages if you don't check your newsgroups frequently enough. How frequently is frequently enough varies from one newsgroup to the next.*

When you click one of these buttons, the newsreader displays the appropriate messages from the newsgroup, as shown in Fig. 5-3.

As you can see if you examine Fig. 5-3 closely, not all the messages that appear in a newsgroup are related to genealogy. The first message in the window, for example, is an advertisement for "FREE" Web space for a business. This type of message, unrelated to the topic of the newsgroup, and usually posted to tens or hundreds of groups, is colloquially known as *spam*.

Figure 5-3

Viewing a list of the messages in a newsgroup.

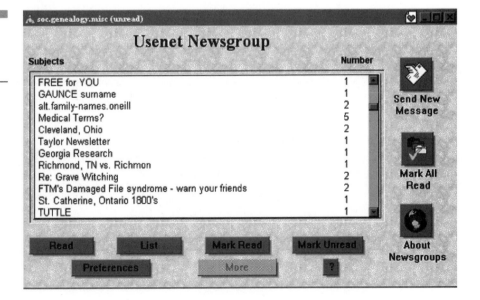

Another advertisement in Fig. 5-3 is more appropriate. That is the one that begins "Taylor Newsletter...". Messages like this are appropriate for a genealogy newsgroup. Before you post a message like this, make sure that it really is a new site that hasn't been discussed in this newsgroup before.

In most unmoderated groups, you'll also find flames, advertisements for pornography, and plain old vulgarity. Just ignore the messages that are inappropriate. This is the price of free speech.

You'll notice that most of the message topics in Fig. 5-3 are actually related to genealogy. To the right of each message topic is a number, usually the number 1. That number tells you how many messages are in that topic's message *thread*. A message thread is a series of messages, all related to the same subject. Threads are generated when people reply to an original message.

As with the window where you selected which newsgroups to read, you have a set of buttons around the list of messages you can read. Here's what each button does for you:

- *Send New Message.*   This button lets you create a new message that will be sent to this newsgroup.

- *Mark All Read.*   When you click this button, the newsreader marks all the messages in this newsgroup as already read. This is useful if you've read all the messages that interest you and aren't interested in reading anything more. If you mark all the messages as read, the next time you open the newsgroup with the **List Unread** button, you'll only see new messages. The older ones that you aren't interested in won't appear.

- *Read.*   This button lets you read the message that is currently selected.

- *List.*   If you click this button, the newsreader will open a window that contains additional information about every message in the selected thread. The information displayed is the e-mail address of the person who posted each message, the size of the message, and the date and time the message was posted.

- *More.*   Click this button to see more topics in the newsgroup. If there are no more topics to see, this button will be dimmed.

- *Mark Read.*   If you know you don't want to read a particular thread, you can select it, then click Mark Read. All the messages in the thread will be treated as if you had already read them. This means they won't appear the next time you look at the newsgroup with the **List Unread** option.

■ *Mark Unread.*   If you know you'll want to reread a particular thread, you can select it, then click **Mark Unread**. All the messages in the thread will be treated as if you had not already read them. This means they'll still appear the next time you look at the newsgroup using the **List Unread** option.

■ *Preferences.*   Use this button to change some of the newsreader settings for this newsgroup. In most cases, the default settings are fine.

■ *About Newsgroups.*   This button actually takes you back to the main newsgroup window, the one you see when you go to the Newsgroups keyword.

When you read a message posted to a newsgroup, you will see a window like the one shown in Fig. 5-4. Following the pattern of other windows in the newsreader, the message you are reading appears in the large, scrollable list box, while the controls are buttons around the edges of this box.

Here's a list of what you can do with these buttons:

Figure 5-4

Reading a message posted to a newsgroup.

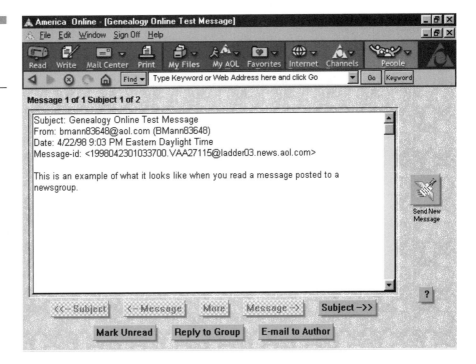

■ *Send New Message.* Use this button when you want to stop reading this message and compose an unrelated one of your own.

■ *Mark Unread.* Use this button to tell the newsreader to treat this message as if you haven't actually read it yet. The message can still appear in the list of unread messages the next time you look at this newsgroup.

■ *Reply to Group.* Click this button if you want to reply to this message with a post to the newsgroup. Your message gets added to the message thread and distributed around the world as part of the newsgroup message traffic.

■ *E-mail to Author.* This button lets you reply to the message you are reading by sending an e-mail message directly to the person who posted the message, and not to the newsgroup.

The other five buttons in this window let you move between messages and topics without leaving the window. They are:

■ *<<—Subject.* This button displays the first message in the thread before this one in the newsgroup. You would then begin reading that thread, and all the commands would be relative to that thread.

■ Subject—>>. This button displays the first message in the thread after this one in the newsgroup. You would then begin reading that thread, and all the commands would be relative to that thread.

■ *<—Message.* Use this button to read the message that preceded the one you are reading now; that is, to read the message that was sent before this one.

■ *Message—>.* Use this button to read the message that came after the one you are reading now; that is, to read the message that is a reply to the one you are reading now.

■ *More.* If the message you are reading is too long to fit into the list box, this button will be active. Click it to see more of the message. Most of the time this button will be dimmed, since most messages will fit into the list box.

Working with Newsgroups Offline

All of the newsgroup activity you've seen so far is done online. That is, you do it all while connected to AOL, with the clock ticking if you are paying by the hour. However, America Online has an option to let you send and retrieve newsgroup messages for offline use.

First, you need to get online and set everything up. Go to the Newsgroups windows and click **Read Offline**. You'll see the Choose Newsgroups window shown in Fig. 5-5.

Initially, the newsgroups you are subscribed to appear in the Subscribed Newsgroups list box on the left. To read a newsgroup offline, select it in the left box, then click the **Add>** button. The newsgroup will move from the left box to the Newsgroups to read offline list box on the right. You can move newsgroups from right to left with the **<Remove** button. And you can move all the newsgroups from one box to the other with the **Add All>>** or **<<Remove All** buttons. Once you have the newsgroups arranged the way you want them, click **OK**.

Now close the Choose Newsgroups window and go to the Automatic AOL window. Automatic AOL is covered in detail under "Automatic AOL" in Chap. 4, but in case you don't remember how to work with it, here is the condensed version of those instructions. Go to the Mail Center, then click **Mail Features**. Click **Automatic AOL** in the menu of features, followed by the **Automatic AOL** icon in the lower right corner of the window. Either work with the Automatic AOL Walk-Through window, or

Figure 5-5

Use the Choose Newsgroups window to select the newsgroups you want to be able to read offline.

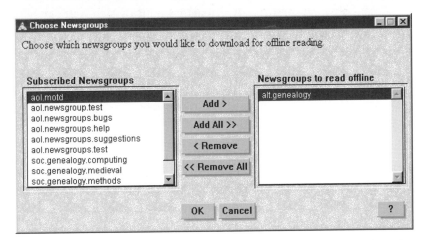

click **Expert Setup** to set everything at once, without help. However you do it, you'll eventually have the option of receiving incoming newsgroup messages and sending outgoing newsgroup messages during Automatic AOL. Select these options, and you're all set. Now whenever a Flash Session runs, you'll get the newsgroups you selected, too. This will make the Automatic AOL longer than if you were just sending and receiving mail, but it's still less online time than reading the newsgroups live.

To read and send messages offline, click **File** on the AOL main menu, then **Personal Filing Cabinet**. In the **Newsgroups** folder, double click the newsgroup messages you want to read. Click **Reply** or **Reply to Author** if you wish to do these things. You can click the **Automatic AOL** button to change your Flash Session settings while reading newsgroup messages.

Now that you know how to subscribe to newsgroups and send or receive messages, you need some newsgroups to explore. The next section will give you some genealogy starting points.

Newsgroups of Interest to Online Genealogists

Once upon a time, there was one online genealogy Usenet news group for genealogy: *soc.roots.* But it became unwieldy to try to discuss beginners' questions, software, history, specific regions, specific family name queries, and the joy we get from our hobby all in one newsgroup. After much discussion, soul-searching, argument, pleading, and finally reconciliation, we now have an embarrassment of riches in genealogical news groups:

alt.adoption—A newsgroup that discusses adoption issues, including the search for birth parents.

alt.genealogy—An older genealogy group, very general, and mostly people who don't want to use *soc.genealogy.misc* for some reason. Gatewayed with the *ALT-GENEALOGY* mailing list.

alt.culture.cajun—A discussion of Cajun history, genealogy, culture, and events.

fido.eur.genealogy—A FidoNet echo copied to Usenet, and meant for those researching European genealogy. FidoNet is a message network for dial-up bulletin board systems.

fido.ger.genealogy—As above, but for German genealogy research, with most messages in German.

fr.rec.genealogie—Gatewayed with the *GEN-FF-L* mailing list for the discussion of Francophone genealogy (the genealogy of French-speaking people). The primary language here is French.

no.slekt—General genealogy topics, with most of the messages in Norwegian. Gatewayed with the *NO.SLEKT* mailing list.

no.slekt.programmer—Discussions of genealogy computer software, with most messages in Norwegian. Gatewayed with the *NO.SLEKT .PROGRAMMER* mailing list.

soc.genealogy.african—For the study of genealogy in Africa and the African diaspora.

soc.genealogy.australia+nz—For genealogical research into Australia, New Zealand, and their territories.

soc.genealogy.benelux—Genealogical discussions of Luxembourg, Belgium, and The Netherlands.

soc.genealogy.computing—About genealogical programs, bugs, and how-to instructions. Mostly about software, with some hardware discussions. Gatewayed with the *SOFTWARE.GENCMP-L* mailing list.

soc.genealogy.french—Genealogy of French-speaking peoples, with most messages in French. Gatewayed with the *GEN-FR-L* mailing list.

soc.genealogy.german—Discussions of family history for anyone with a Germany background. Messages are mainly in German. Gatewayed with the *GEN-DE-L* mailing list.

soc.genealogy.hispanic—Genealogy discussions as related to Hispanics, including Central and South America, with many messages in Spanish.

soc.genealogy.jewish—A moderated discussion of Judaic genealogy. Gatewayed with the *JEWISHGEN* mailing list.

soc.genealogy.marketplace—Buy, sell, trade books; read about programs, seminars, and so on related to genealogy.

soc.genealogy.medieval—Gatewayed with the *GEN-MEDIEVAL* mailing list for genealogy and family history discussions among people researching individuals living during medieval times. Medieval times are loosely defined as the period from the breakup of the Western Roman Empire until the time public records relating to the general population began to be kept, and extending roughly from A.D. 500 to A.D. 1600.

soc.genealogy.methods—A general discussion of genealogy and methods of genealogical research. Gatewayed to the *GENMTD-L* mailing list.

soc.genealogy.misc—This is what became of *soc.roots*. It is a general discussion of genealogy. Gatewayed into the *GENMSC-L* mailing list, it is a list for topics that don't fit into other *soc.genealogy.* categories.

soc.genealogy.nordic—Genealogical products and services for Northern Europe.

soc.genealogy.slavic—Slavic genealogy. Some messages in Slavic languages.

soc.genealogy.surnames.global—A central database for sending queries about surnames from around the world. This newsgroup is moderated.

soc.genealogy.uk+ireland—Gatewayed with the *GENUKI-L* mailing list for the discussion of genealogy and family history. Also for discussions among people researching ancestors, family members, or others who have a genealogical connection to any people in any part of the British Isles (England, Wales, Ireland, Scotland, the Channel Isles, and the Isle of Man).

soc.genealogy.west-indies—Caribbean genealogy; most but not all of the messages are in English.

In addition, are several groups in the *soc.history.* hierarchy that discuss areas touching on issues genealogists face: records, sources, and so on.

Binary Files on Usenet

Some newsgroups carry binary files; they have the word "binaries" in their names. This isn't seen so much on Usenet any more because the World Wide Web is far superior for trading sounds, pictures, and programs; still, sometimes people do encode a binary file, which has nontext characters, into ASCII codes that can transfer on Usenet. This is called Uuencoding or binary encoding.

When you first join AOL, your account is set to the default of blocking all binary files in Usenet, because most of the groups that send binaries are pornographic. To change this setting go to Keyword Parental Controls, click on **Set Parental Controls Now**, click on **Custom Controls**, and click on **Newsgroups**. Click on **Newsgroups Controls** and **Edit**. Choose the Screen Name. Uncheck the **Block binary downloads** box.

Encoded binary files are often broken up across several different messages. Gathering up the pieces, putting them together, and converting them back to original form used to be a real hassle. America Online's File-Grabber feature makes it very simple.

To get the most out of this, set the **Complete Binaries Only** preference. In the Usenet window, click **Read My Newsgroups**. Click on a newsgroup name in your list that contains the word *binary* or *binaries* to select it. Click the **Preferences** button and select the **Complete Binaries Only** preference. *Note:* You have to do this newsgroup by newsgroup; this setting is not available in the Global Newsgroups Prefences window.

AOL's newsreader alerts you when you are viewing encoded data, and gives you three choices: Download the file (and the AOL software will automatically decode it for you); download the article that contains the code or piece of it (and you decode the pieces yourself); or cancel.

Newsgroup FAQ Files

Many newsgroups post files of information called Frequently Asked Questions (FAQs). About once a month, these get posted to their own newsgroup and to the newsgroup *soc.answers.* Look for a message called the Meta Genealogy FAQ, posted about the 22nd of each month to most of the *soc.genealogy* newsgroups; this message will show you how to get the FAQ files for the individual genealogy newsgroups.

Searching for Information Within Newsgroups

You don't always have to read the whole newsgroup to find the information you need. There are several places where you can search newsgroups one or several or all at a time. As an America Online user, the logical place for you to start is AOL's NetFind. NetFind can search newsgroups, either the messages (called articles in NetFind) or the newsgroup descriptions. For a full run-down on NetFind, skip to Chap. 7, "AOL NetFind and Other Search Engines."

Other useful tools for searching for specific information within newsgroups are InfoSeek (http://www.infoseek.com) and DejaNews. Both of these tools are covered in detail in Chap. 7.

CHAPTER 6

The World
Wide Web

The World Wide Web (a.k.a. the Web, or WWW) is probably what you think of when you think of the Internet. The Web is the part of the Internet with all the fancy graphics and sound. The World Wide Web is also the easiest part of the Internet to use—just point to something with the mouse and click on it.

NOTE   *America Online's software comes with a version of Microsoft Internet Explorer as its Web browser. This is great for you, since Internet Explorer is a fast, powerful browser.*

The Web is also a great resource for online genealogists. Much of the growth of the Internet over the last few years has been in the Web. Thousands of Web sites spring up every month. Many people, particularly newcomers to the Internet, don't even use any other part of the Internet.

As you might imagine, any place on the Internet that combines ease of use, lots of excitement, and lots of new people is a place genealogists will want to be. You can find hundreds of Web sites of interest to genealogists. In this chapter we identify 50 good ones for you to start with.

What Does the World Wide Web Look Like?

You may not realize it, but you've almost certainly seen the Web before. With all the hype and excitement about the Internet, the Web, and the material available through them, pictures from the Web are constantly showing up on TV and in newspapers, magazines, and books. Plus, if you've been reading this book from cover to cover, you've already seen several figures showing Web pages, and may already have ventured out onto the Web. But, just so everyone is clear, Fig. 6-1 shows a Web page, the Genealogy Home Page, as displayed by the version of Internet Explorer built into the AOL software. The URL for this page is http://www.genhomepage.com/.

█ █ █ █ █ █ █ █

Figure 6-1
The Genealogy Home
Page as displayed by
the Internet Explorer
Web browser built into
current AOL software.

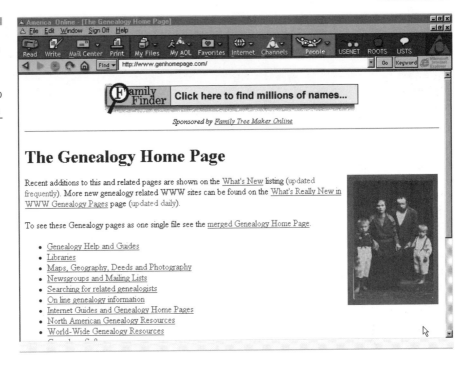

How Browsers Work

The World Wide Web has its own lexicon of terminology, which can be confusing. Here are a few terms you should know before you get going.

- ■ *HTML (Hypertext Markup Language).* This language turns a text document into one that can be viewed on the World Wide Web.

- ■ *HTTP (Hypertext Transfer Protocol).* This set of rules governs how information transfers on the World Wide Web. The letters *http* appear as the access method in every full Web address (URL).

- ■ *Session.* A Web session is the entire period of time from when the user starts his or her Web browser until the user ends his or her time online.

- ■ *URL (Uniform Resource Locator).* An address in the Internet. The format of a URL is access method://machine.name/directory/file. (Example: http://www.genhomepage.com/.) Access method can be FTP, http, gopher, or any other Internet service. The machine name is the com-

puter that holds what you are after. The directory and file are where
the object is on that computer . You type the URL in your browser's
address box to get there.

■ A *page* is a file presented to you in the browser. The file will be simple
ASCII text, with embedded HTML commands to tell the browser
how things should look to you. Some text will be designated a "headline," other text might tell the browser to show a picture in a certain
place. The first page you see when you visit a Web site is usually
called the home page.

■ A *link* is a pointer to another file. The term for a system of linked
information is *hypertext*. Hypertext, as found on the Web, is a system
whereby pointers are embedded in text—presented to you usually as
underlined colored words or a picture—that will have the browser
display another file either on that same site or somewhere else on the
Internet. When the cursor changes from an arrow to a hand, you are
pointing your mouse at a link.

If you click on a link, you will be taken to another document, perhaps at another site, that has information on your choice. Or the
browser may show you a picture, play a song, run a video clip, or whatever. In each case, however, the browser is merely following the link to
another file, then taking actions that are appropriate for that file.

NOTE   *Depending on the speed of your connection to America Online (see the
information on modems in Chap. 1), all the fancy features of the Web could slow
down your research. By the end of this chapter, you'll learn several tips for speed-
ing up World Wide Web access by controlling how AOL's browser handles things
like sound and graphics.*

What is wonderful about the Web is that most browsers (including the
one that comes built into current AOL software) combine many Internet
services: sending and receiving e-mail, reading and posting to Usenet,
transferring files with ftp and gopher, and subscribing to mailing lists.

How AOL's Browser Works

America Online has worked hard to enhance your Internet experience.
One of the ways they have done this is by replacing the old AOL Web
browser with a version of Microsoft Internet Explorer (IE). With IE as

your Web browser, you're well equipped for virtually any genealogy site or resource you'll run into or dig up.

For ease of reference, Fig. 6-2 once again shows you the AOL IE Web browser window. To get here, you can click the **Internet** menu in the tool-bar, choosing **Internet Connection** from the drop-down menu, or you can use the keyword Internet. But the simplest way is to type a URL in the address box in the AOL window. Type in http://www.aol.com and you will get the same page you would using the menu or keyword, as in Fig. 6-2.

In Fig. 6-2, you can see the browser's title bar at the top of the screen. This is where IE displays the title of the Web page you're viewing. The title is often the same as the page's first headline, but it can be different.

On the right side of the title bar is a small icon of a piece of paper with a red heart on it. This is the **Favorite Places** icon. Click it to add the current Web page to your list of favorite places or to insert the URL in an instant message or mail message to a friend.

When you save a Web page's address (URL) in your **Favorite Places** folder, the name associated with the URL is taken from the title bar. Sadly, many Web developers don't take advantage of this, and name their pages something uninformative such as My Page or Link.

Figure 6-2
The Internet Explorer Web browser built into AOL software has relatively few controls and settings, making it easy to work with.

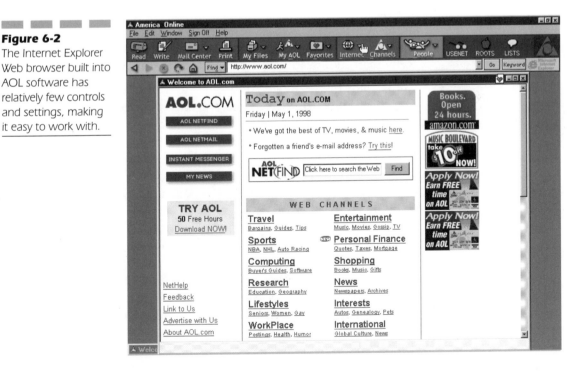

Next to the **Address** box are some buttons, which you can use to control the AOL Web browser. If a button won't do anything in a particular situation, that button is dimmed. Here's a description of each button and what it does.

- *Back Button.* This left-pointing triangle button takes you to the previous page you visited this session.

- *Forward Button.* This button takes you to the page you viewed *after* you viewed the currently visible one. This can happen if you've used the **Back** button this session.

- *Stop Button.* Click this button to stop a page from downloading. There are several reasons why you might do this, the most common being that a page that is taking too long to download.

- *Reload Button.* This button makes the browser reload the current Web page. You might want to do this if a page seems to be loading slowly or not at all. You might also want to do this if you have reason to believe that the page has changed since you started looking at it this session (say a weather site).

- *Home Button.* This brings you to the page you have configured as your home page, the place the browser automatically goes to when you start it.

- *Find Button.* This button has three options: Find it on AOL, Find it on the Web (takes you to AOL NetFind, an Internet search engine that allows you to search the Web and newsgroups, as well as e-mail and postal mail address information), and Find AOL Access numbers.

To the right of the toolbar is a blue AOL logo. When the browser is downloading something from the Internet, this logo spins. When the logo stops spinning, the download is complete.

Underneath the toolbar is the Address bar. This is where you can enter URLs you want to visit. It's also where IE displays the URL of the current page. At the right end of the Address bar is a down arrow. Click this arrow to see a list of the last 15 or so URLs (or AOL areas) you have visited.

The Status bar is at the bottom of the IE window, on the left side. In it, messages appear describing what the browser is doing at any given moment, or what URL the browser is displaying. Move your mouse pointer over links on a page and you'll see the associated URLs displayed here, too. If the site's developer is versed in the Java programming language, a message can scroll across the status bar like a ticker tape. On the bottom right side is a bar that portrays what percentage of a file upload or download has been completed so far.

You're almost ready to start exploring the list of genealogy Web sites we've provided for you. Before you go, take a look at the browser tips and tricks we've collected for you. Master them, and you'll spend less time fiddling with your browser and more time doing genealogy.

Browser Tips and Tricks

There are ways to use your browser to better surf the World Wide Web. This list contains some of the most valuable tips available:

- The AOL version of the Microsoft Internet Explorer will input the http:// for you if you type in the unique part of the address. For example, type www.genhomepage.com and the browser will add the http:// for you.

- Type in an address that begins with the letters FTP (ftp.symantec.com, for example), and the browser will insert the necessary ftp://. (An FTP site is a collection of files for public download.)

- If you need to copy a URL to your clipboard, you can just click in the **Address** box, press **CTRL-C**, and you have a copy of the URL that's ready to be pasted elsewhere. This can be useful if you want to make reference to the URL in another program.

- You can change your browser home page (the page IE opens when you start a session) by opening the page you want as your new home page and clicking **MY AOL**, then **Preferences**. Click the **WWW** button and the Internet Options window will appear. On the **General** tab, in the **Home Page** section of the tab, click **Use Current**. This will make IE treat the page you are viewing at the time as your home page. You can click **Use Default** on the same tabbed sheet to restore www.aol.com as your browser home page.

- Click the down arrow in the Address box to see a list of the URLs you've visited recently. This comes in very handy if you can't remember how to get back to a particularly neat site you visited recently.

- Because of a slow modem or lack of patience, you may not want to wait for graphics or other multimedia effects to load. The good news is you can turn them off. The bad news is that you must do it outside of AOL. On your desktop is an icon for Microsoft Internet Explorer. Right click it and choose **Properties**. Choose the **Advanced** tab. Scroll down to the section on Multimedia. Uncheck **Show pictures** to turn off graphics in the browser. (You can set or clear any of the multimedia options from here). Only do this as a last resort. The World Wide Web is a multimedia place, and turning off all your multimedia options can make it harder and less enjoyable to use. Figure 6-3 shows what the AOL.com page looks like with all its multimedia options turned off.

- If you forgot to bookmark a site, and the URL list in the Address box doesn't help, you can take a look in your **History** folder. IE keeps a history of all the sites and pages you've visited recently. By default, it keeps track of the last 20 days for you. You can go to the History folder and rummage around if you think seeing the name of the Web site will get you on the right track. Here's how you do it:

  1. Using Windows Explorer, find the **History** folder in the Windows directory.
  2. Double click the **History** folder. You'll see a collection of Calendar folders as in Fig. 6-4.
  3. Double click a **Calendar** folder. Inside the folder you'll see Site folders.

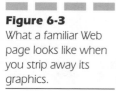

Figure 6-3
What a familiar Web page looks like when you strip away its graphics.

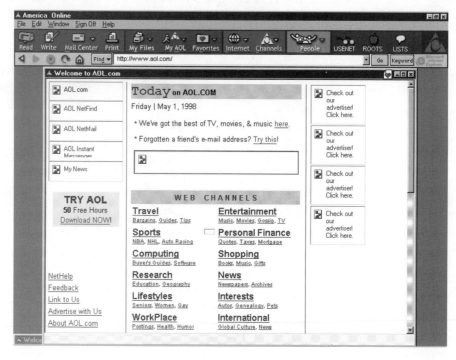

Figure 6-4
See where you've
been on the Internet
recently by looking in
the Calendar folders
Internet Explorer
creates for you.

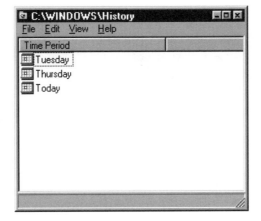

4. Double click a **Site** folder to see links to all the pages you've visited recently at that Web site.

5. Double click a link to go to that Web page.

■ All browsers save copies of the text, pictures, and other files you see in your Web browser window. They use these stored files the next time you visit the site, loading the ones on your disk if they are the same as the ones at the remote site, for faster display. If you are running low on disk space on your PC, you can delete these files. Web pages may take a little longer to load, but you'll free a ton of space on your hard drive. To do this, click **My AOL** and choose **Preferences**, then **WWW**. On the **General** tab, in the Temporary Internet Files section of the tabbed sheet, click **Delete Files**.

Four Score and Seven Sites to See

Since the first publication of this book, the number of genealogy-related Web pages has gone from a handful to literally thousands. And with the rate at which things appear, disappear, and change location on the Internet, you'll never be able to see them all. So how do you find genealogy sites that are worth seeing? We have the answer. To make things easier for you, we've found 87 Web sites that are good starting places for online genealogists. Not all of these sites address genealogy specifically, but they can all be of use in your research.

We considered these factors:

- Timeliness—how the site is updated, and kept accurate
- Usefulness—how well it matches the needs of genealogists
- Uniqueness—information not found elsewhere, or presented in a unique manner
- Organization—how easy it is to find and retrieve the information there

In the manner of Web sites everywhere, these sites will all lead you to other sites, eventually (we hope) leading you to exactly the information you need. Realize that this isn't even close to an exhaustive list; for that, see Cyndi's List and Genealogy Resources on the Internet, listed below. In the list that follows, the sites are listed alphabetically, not ranked.

NOTE   *All of these links were active when we wrote this. With the rate at which things change on the Web, it's likely that at least some links you find here will be gone by the time you read this. That's just the way things go on the Web.*

1. Acadian Genealogy Homepage (http://www.acadian.org/) contains information about French Acadian and French Canadian genealogy, and includes ordering information for a CD-ROM covering over half a million people of almost exclusively French Acadian/French Canadian ancestry.

2. Afrigeneas Home Page (http://www.msstate.edu/Archives/History/afrigen/index.html) is the starting place for African-American family history. Don't miss our in-depth profile of this site later in the chapter.

3. Allen County (Indiana) Public Library Historical Genealogy Department (http://www.acpl.lib.in.us/genealogy/genealogy.html) has over 220,000 printed volumes, 251,000 microfilms and microfiches, and 38,000 volumes of compiled genealogies in their collection. They also have census data going back to the 1700s, city directories, passenger lists, military records, Native American, African American, and many other sets of records. If you ever want to do a genealogy road trip, consider putting this library on your itinerary.

4. American Civil War Home Page (http://sunsite.utk.edu/civil-war/) has links to fantastic online documents from all sort of sources, including two academics who have made the Civil War their career.

5. Ancestry Inc.'s Discovering Your Heritage (http://www.ancestry.com/ dyh/intro2.html) is a basic beginner's how-to information source on genealogy.

6. AOL Hispanic Genealogy Special Interest Group (http://users.aol .com/mrosado007/) is the gathering place for a group of Hispanic genealogists on America Online. Links include a newsletter, heraldry information, a surname list, and more.

7. Archaic Words & Phrases (http://home.sprynet.com/sprynet/lgk71/ 2archaic.htm) is a list of some words and phrases that once had meanings different than as used today.

8. Bob Fieg's (http://www.getnet.com/~bfieg/) is a typical personal home page, but with genealogy and pedigree chart software.

9. British Heraldic Archive, The (http://www.kwtelecom.com/heraldry/) is dedicated to increasing interest in heraldry, genealogy, chivalry, and related topics.

10. Calendars (http://home.sprynet.com/sprynet/lgk71/2calenda.htm) is an explanation of the transition from the Julian to the Gregorian calendar, which occurred in 1752.

11. Canadian Genealogy Sources (http://www.iosphere.net/~jholwell/ cangene/main.html) will get you started in Canadian genealogical research. The flags on the page are for each Canadian province. Click on the proper flag icon for resources in that province.

12. Canadian Heritage Information Network (http://www.chin.gc.ca/) is a bilingual (French or English) guide to museums, galleries, and other heritage-oriented resources in Canada. Figure 6-5 shows the home page of this site.

13. Carrie's Adoptee & Genealogy Page (http://www.mtjeff.com/ ~bodenst/page3.html) offers links to resources for adoption, German heritage, and general genealogy.

14. Census Bureau Home Page (http://www.census.gov/) has a list of Frequently Occurring Names in the US for 1990, Spanish surname list for 1990, an age search service, and a Frequently Asked Questions (FAQ) file on genealogy.

15. CLIO—The National Archives Information Server—Genealogy (http://www.nara.gov/genealogy/genindex.html) lists genealogy holdings of the United States National Archives. You can find information on their Quick Guides to genealogy topics, check a catalog of Aids for Genealogical Research, look at the NARA Book Store, use

Figure 6-5
This site is a one-stop guide to museums, galleries, and other heritage-oriented resources in Canada.

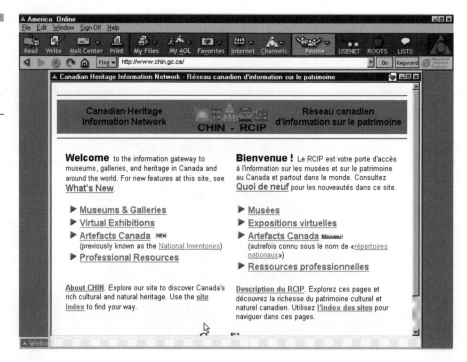

the Soundex machine to find the Soundex code for your surnames, and much more.

16. Cyndi's List of Genealogy Sites on the Internet (http://www .cyndislist.com/) is the best organized and annotated list of WWW genealogy sites. A must see!

17. David Eppstein's home page (http://www.ics.uci.edu/~eppstein/gene/) has information on his shareware program Gene for the Macintosh.

18. Dead Person's Society, Melbourne, Victoria, Australia (http://avoca .vicnet.net.au/~dpsoc/) contains valuable information for people researching Australia and New Zealand. Includes old place names, wills, diaries, and more.

19. Directory of Royal Genealogical Data (http://www.dcs.hull.ac.uk/ public/genealogy/royal/catalog.html) is a database containing the genealogy of the British Royal family and many of the other ruling families of the Western world (they seem to have all been interrelated somehow). Contains over 18,000 names.

20. Dott's Genealogy Home Page (http://home.att.net/~dottsr/) has lots of great info on Iowa and Ohio resources.

21. Eastman's Online Genealogy Newsletter (http://www.ancestry.com/home/eastarch.htm) is a weekly all-text newsletter on genealogy topics. A typical issue will cover reviews of genealogy computer programs; news items of note to genealogists; a list of Web sites to visit; book, CD-ROM, and TV reviews; and more.

22. Everton's Guide to Genealogy on the World Wide Web (http://www.everton.com/) including an online version of the venerable Helper. Links to online resources, tutorial for genealogy beginners; test-drive their genealogical database On-Line Search.

23. Family Chronicle (http://www.familychronicle.com/) is the Web site for this magazine, which is dedicated to families researching their roots. Check out their offerings and request a free sample of the magazine.

24. Family History, How Do I Begin (http://www.lds.org/Family_History/How_Do_I_Begin.html) is the Church of Jesus Christ of Latter-Day Saints' basic tutorial.

25. Family TreeMaker Online (http://www.familytreemaker.com/) boasts the FamilyFinder Index, which has genealogy data from users of their programs: 153 million names you can search, the Internet Family-Finder, and Genealogy How-To, a 1200-page guide to genealogy. This site is by Broderbund Software, the publishers of Family Tree Maker.

26. Gathering of the Clans Home Page (http://www.tartans.com/) is described as a reference for people researching the Scottish clans. Includes information on 65 clans, as well as specifically Scottish genealogical resources. See Fig. 6-6.

27. GENDEX (http://www.gendex.com/) is the home site of the GENDES and GED 2HTML software. When you use GED2HTML to post your genealogy on the Web, you can register to be part of the worldwide GENDEX, a search engine for all such genealogy sites.

28. Genealogical Dictionaries (http://home.navisoft.com/scrolls/dictinry.htm), despite the name, is actually a pair of dictionaries that give the English translations of old German terms for occupations and causes of death.

29. Genealogy Dictionary (http://home.att.net/~dottsr/diction.html#DICT), part of Dott's Home Page, is for all those confusing terms such as *cordwainer* and *primogeniture*.

30. Genealogy for Teachers (http://www.execpc.com/~dboals/geneo.html) lists resources, organizations, guides, and tutorials. Aimed at educators, it would help any beginner.

Figure 6-6
If you are of Scottish descent, you should check this site out.

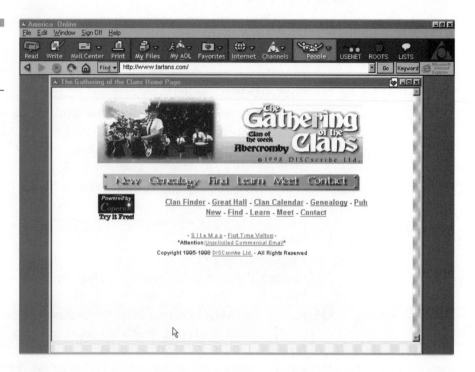

31. Genealogy Gateway to the Web (http://www.polaris.net/~legend/ genalogy.htm) is a collection of links to free genealogical services as well as over 29,000 online resources. The site is sponsored by the Family Tree Maker Online.

32. Genealogy Home Page (http://www.genhomepage.com/) is a wide-ranging index of genealogy resources on the Internet. It includes links to maps, libraries, software, and societies. This site, which is sponsored by Family Tree Maker Online, is examined in detail later in this chapter.

33. Genealogy of the Royal Family of the Netherlands (http://www .xs4all.nl/~tkvenjb/gennl.htm) is a detailed genealogical history of the House of Orange-Nassau. Covers from Heinrich the Rich of Nassau (born 1180) to Juliana Guillermo (born 1981).

34. Genealogy on the Web Ring (http://www.geocities.com/Heartland/ Plains/5270/webring.html) is a group of genealogy Web pages and sites, all connected one to the other in a giant ring. From this page, you can explore the ring's sites in sequence, or select random jumps to put some serendipity (wonderful surprises) into your research.

35. Genealogy Online (http://genealogy.emcee.com/) is a site that provides many resources for online genealogists, including an online copy of the 1880 U.S. census, links to other resources, and Web site hosting.

36. Genealogy Resources on the Internet (http://members.aol.com/johnf14246/internet.html) is an AOL member's site that provides you with a quality sorted list for finding just the genealogical information you are looking for.

37. GenServ—Genealogical Server Information (http://www.genserv.com) is the GenServ's home page and includes general information and how to register. GenServ is covered in detail in App. A.

38. GENUKI (http://midas.ac.uk/genuki/). All about Genealogy in the United Kingdom and Ireland.

39. GenWeb Database Index (http://www.gentree.com/) has links to all known genealogical databases searchable through the Web. Now includes GenDex, an index of name databases with over two million entries.

40. GENWEB Discussion List (http://demo.genweb.org/genweblist/genweblist.html) contains discussions about the GenWeb database. The GenWeb list closed in August 1997, but you can read the discussions that led to its creation here.

41. Global: Everything for the Family Historian (http://www.globalgenealogy.com/) is the Global Genealogy Supply Web site. Shop online for genealogy supplies (maps, forms, software, etc.) and subscribe to the Global Gazette, a free e-mail newsletter covering Canadian genealogy and heritage.

42. HIR—Hungarian Information Resources Genealogy Page (http://mineral.umd.edu/HyperNews/get/hungarian-american-genealogy.html) is a place to start if your research leads you to Hungary. Primarily links to other sites with Hungary-specific genealogical information.

43. How to Get Past Genealogy Road Blocks (http://www.firstct.com/fv/stone.html) is a quick refresher on what to do when you are just plain stuck, and can't get past, over, around, or through that brick wall.

44. International Research (http://www.intl-research.com/) is an association of accredited genealogists who will, for a fee, do your genealogical research for you. A place to go if you are really stuck.

45. Isleuth—Arts & Humanities—Genealogy (http://www.isleuth.com/gene.html) is a place to search for genealogical resources. ISLEUTH

(Fig. 6-7) connects to lots of online databases for you: selected census records, Social Security Death Index, British Columbia Cemeteries, and more.

46. Italian Genealogy Home Page (http://www.italgen.com/) has chat forums, databases, tips, and a toolbox for researching Italian family names.

47. Janyce's Root Diggin' Dept. (http://www.janyce.com/gene/rootdig .html) is yet another good place for beginners to start their online genealogical research.

48. JewishGen (http://wwwl.jewishgen.org/) is a comprehensive resource for researchers of Jewish genealogy worldwide. Among other things, it includes the JewishGen Family Finder, a database of towns and surnames being researched by Jewish genealogists worldwide, and can be searched on the WWW or via e-mail (e-mail the server commands; results are e-mailed back to you).

49. Journal of Online Genealogy (http://www.onlinegenealogy.com/) is a monthly Web-based newsletter about genealogy. Includes links to many other online genealogy resources.

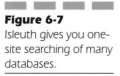

Figure 6-7
Isleuth gives you one-site searching of many databases.

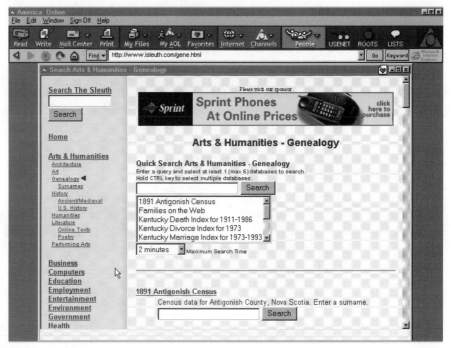

50. Library of Congress (http://www.loc.gov/) is the Web connection to the U.S. government's vast collection of historical documents and other resources. There's plenty of information on how to tap into this monstrous resource later in the chapter.

51. Library of Virginia Digital Collections (http://image.vtls.com/) is a starting point where you can search Virginia colonial records as well as Bible records, newspapers, court records, and state documents.

52. Lineages, Inc. (http://www.lineages.com/default.asp) is the Web site for a group of professional genealogical researchers who will help you find your roots for a fee. In addition, this site includes some free information, such as "First Steps for Beginners," a free genealogical queries page, and more.

53. List of Genealogy Bulletin Board Systems—Home Page (http://www.genealogy.org/~gbbs/) lists every dial-up BBS that carries FIDOnet genealogy echoes, and it's searchable!

54. Marston Manor (http://www.geocities.com/Heartland/Plains/1638/) is a site that offers numerous useful items for online genealogists, including a chart for calculating family relationships and a detailed discussion of the terms *proof* and *evidence* as they relate to genealogy.

55. Marvelicious Genealogy (http://www.marvelcreations.com/genealogybkmk.html) is an extensive and visually striking (see Fig. 6-8) collection of genealogy links.

56. Mayflower Web Pages (http://users.aol.com/calebj/mayflower.html) contains the passenger lists of the *Mayflower, Fortune,* and *Anne,* plus many related documents.

57. Medal of Honor Citations (http://www.army.mil/cmh-pg/mohl.htm) contains the names and text of the citations for the more than 3400 people who have been awarded the Congressional Medal of Honor since 1861.

58. National Genealogical Society (http://www.genealogy.org/~ngs/) is the granddaddy of all genealogical societies. Here, you'll find announcements of NGS seminars, workshops, and programs, as well as information on NGS's home study course, youth resources, and other activities. This is an excellent site for learning genealogy standards and methods.

59. Native American Genealogy (http://members.aol.com/bbbenge/front.html) is an AOL-based site that tries to keep up with the latest in sites and resources for Native Americans.

Figure 6-8
Lots of links
and a beautiful
presentation make
Marvelicious
Genealogy a
worthwhile stop
during your research.

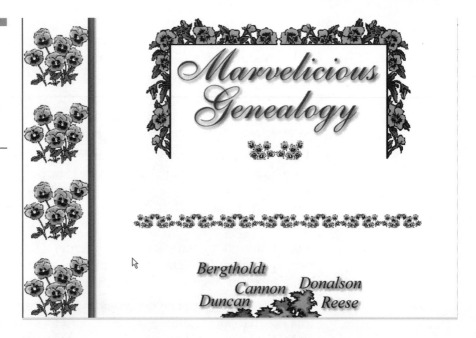

60. New England Historic Genealogical Society (http://www.nehgs.org/) is designed to be a center for family and local history research in New England. The Society owns 200,000 genealogy books and documents. If you are a New England genealogist, you should check them out.

61. Oregon History & Genealogy Resources (http://www.rootsweb.com/~genepool/oregon.htm) is a collection of genealogy information for Oregon, with links to the wider world of genealogy sites as well.

62. Our Spanish Heritage: History and Genealogy of South Texas and Northeast Mexico (http://www.geocities.com/Heartland/Ranch/5442/) is an interesting source if you're looking for relatives from the South Texas/Northeast Mexico area. The database has over 11,000 names, all interrelated as lineages.

63. Pitcairn Island Web Site (http://www.wavefront.com/~pjlareau/bounty1.html) is the place to find information about the current inhabitants of Pitcairn Island. But more importantly for genealogists, this is the place to go to get information on over 7500 descendants of the crew of the HMS *Bounty,* of *Mutiny on the Bounty* fame.

64. Poland Worldgenweb (http://www.rootsweb.com/~polwgw/polandgen.html) has maps and other information on Polish

provinces, as well as a surname search. You can also adopt a province, becoming the provider of information about it.

65. Quick Guide to Genealogy in Ireland (http://www.bess.tcd.ie/roots/ prototyp/qguide.htm) is a beginner's guide to Irish genealogical resources.

66. RAND Genealogy Club Home Page (http://www.rand.org:80/ personal/Genea/) lets you search Roots Surnames and Locations and get Soundex codes.

67. Repositories of Primary Sources (http://www.uidaho.edu/special-collections/Other.Repositories.html) is a listing of over 2500 Web sites describing holdings of manuscripts, archives, rare books, historical photographs, and other primary sources. It's worth a look.

68. ROOTS-L Page (http://www.rootsweb.com/roots-l) is the home page of the ROOTS-L mailing list.

69. RootsComputing (http://www.rootscomputing.com/) is a categorized guide to genealogy on the WWW. It's another great starting place, and we examine it in detail later in the chapter.

70. Scrapbooking Idea Network Genealogy Links page (http://www .scrapbooking.com/linksgenealogy.htm) has information on how to preserve your family history once you create it.

71. Social Security Death Index (http://www.ancestry.com/ssdi/ advanced.htm) is a tool that allows you to search the Social Security Administration's records for birth and death dates of deceased Americans. Other information includes Social Security Number, last known residence, and more.

72. South Carolina Library (http://www.sc.edu/library/socar/books .html) is an online card catalog for the South Carolina Library, which houses an extensive collection of genealogy holdings.

73. Spanish Heritage home page (http://members.aol.com/shhar/), an AOL-based site, is the home of the Society of Hispanic Historical and Ancestral Research™.

74. Surnames.com (http://www.surnames.com/) has genealogy in general, Arizona in particular. It includes a surname search and a map of genealogical organizations in the United States. The site also has a useful beginner's section.

75. Surnames: What's in a Name? (http://clanhuston.com/name/name .htm) is a large collection of surnames and their meanings. (The site describes the list as "fairly extensive—but it certainly isn't all-

inclusive.") There is also a brief history of surnames, with references.

76. Swiss Genealogy Project (http://www.mindspring.com/~philipp/che .html) is a set of pages for researching Swiss genealogy, maintained by a group of volunteers. It includes several maps with detailed information on each district.

77. Tracking Your Roots (http://members.aol.com/GenWebLisa/) is an AOL-based gold mine of Alabama genealogy information, county by county. The Tennessee River, which flows through North Alabama, was a major westward immigration route from Tennessee, Virginia, and the Carolinas. We'll give you the full lowdown on this site later in the chapter.

78. Traveller Southern Families (http://www.traveller.com/genealogy/) (Fig. 6-9), dedicated to the genealogy of Southern Families, Civil War Pages, Government Web Servers, Genealogy Software Companies, Family Societies and/or Associations Pages, Books for Sale, and Genealogy Newsgroups.

79. Treasure Maps, the How-to Genealogy Site (http://www.firstct.com/ fv/tmapmenu.html) is one of the best sites on the Web for novices. It

Figure 6-9
If you are researching the American South, you'll want to visit Traveller Southern Families.

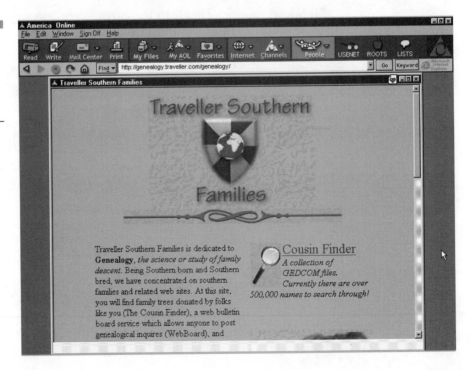

is aimed at hands-on, how-to information to help you actually do research online: tutorials on writing queries, using the U.S. Census, and more. To keep track of the latest news on Treasure Maps, you might want to subscribe to their monthly newsletter.

80. U.S. Gazetteer (http://www.census.gov/cgi-bin/gazetteer). Just type in a city and/or state, and a map will appear showing the location. This service is run by the U.S. Census Bureau, and uses information from the 1990 Census.

81. USGenWeb Project (http://www.usgenweb.org). This is a noncommercial project with the goal of providing a Web site for genealogical research in every county and every state of the United States. There is much more information on this project later in the chapter.

82. Utah State Archives (http://www.archives.state.ut.us/). Click on the **Research Center** for the Archives' public services, which include research, answering questions, and sending you records. Not everything here is free, but it's very convenient!

83. Viet Nam Casualty Search Page (http://www.no-quarter.org/) is a noncommercial site that provides information about American casualties (people killed in action) during the Vietnam War.

84. Xerox Map Server (http://pubweb.parc.xerox.com/map) offers interactive maps for finding anyplace in the world.

85. Yahoo Genealogy Page (http://www.yahoo.com/Arts/Humanities/History/Genealogy/) is a huge collection of links to guides, resources and personal genealogies on Web sites. It includes links to related resources as well.

86. Yale Libraries Gopher (gopher://libgopher.yale.edu/1) is a listing of online card catalogs around the world.

87. Yukon and Alaska History (yukonalaska.tqn.com) offers a range of historical and genealogical information on the Yukon, Alaska, and the people who ventured there. This site is part of The Mining Company Web (a collection of sites with expert guidance on specific subjects).

In-Depth Explorations of Some Major Genealogy Web Sites

While one of the common joys of genealogy and Web browsing is the joy of discovery, some sites deserve guided tours. These sites are particularly interesting or useful to online genealogists, and each one has something in particular we want to be sure you'll know about. However, if you want to discover everything yourself, you have more than enough information to spend years researching online. Just skip past the rest of this section and be on your way.

Genealogy Home Page (http://genhomepage.com/)

The Genealogy Home Page is a wide-ranging index of genealogy resources on the Internet. It includes links to maps, libraries, software, and societies. Right from the start, you can see that this site is more of a guide to the genealogy resources available on the Web than a direct source of genealogical information. The home page (shown in Fig. 6-1) starts off with two links to new, or newly discovered, genealogy sites. There is a URL Suggestion Form at http://www.genhomepage.com/mail.html (Fig. 6-10) that allows you to submit a URL for inclusion on the Genealogy

Figure 6-10

Anyone can use this form to submit new, or newly discovered, genealogy Web sites to the Genealogy Home Page.

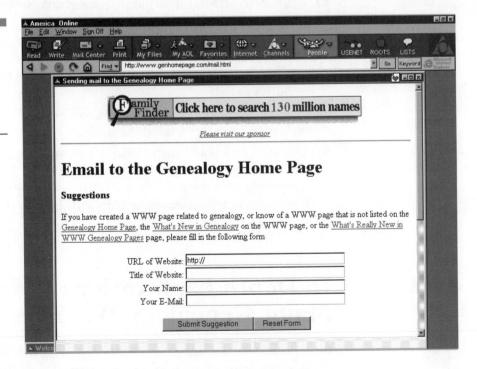

Home Page. If you decide to create your own genealogy Web site (see "Publishing Your Own Genealogy Web Page with AOL Personal Publisher"), this is one way you can announce it to the world.

One of the most useful sections of the Genealogy Home Page is its collection of links under the heading "Genealogy Help and Guides" (http://www.genhomepage.com/help.html). When we were writing this, there were eleven specific resources listed. Here are some of them:

- The ROOTS-L Library link takes you to documents from the famous ROOTS-L mailing list. For everyone from the beginner to the grizzled genealogy veteran, this library has information you need.

- Getting Started in Genealogy and Family History is another useful beginner's guide. If you are into printed documents as well as the computer screen, this guide includes an annotated bibliography of print references.

- Serendipity will give you a lift when the amount of work involved in researching your roots seems overwhelming. It is a collection of stories describing serendipitous genealogical discoveries others have made.

Another set of useful links from the Genealogy Home Page is on the Genealogy Societies page at http://www.genhomepage.com/societies.html. Here you'll find direct links to more than 30 genealogical societies, divided into three categories:

- **Umbrella Organizations** are groups like the Federation of Genealogical Societies.

- **Geographic, National, Ethnic, ... based Societies** covers groups like the American-French Genealogical Society and The Computer Genealogy Society of San Diego.

- **Family-based Societies** are organizations dedicated to research on specific surnames, like the Brown Family Genealogical Society or the Pelletier Family Association.

Afrigeneas (http://www.msstate.edu/Archives/History/afrigen/index.html)

Afrigeneas is a mailing list for African ancestry and genealogical research into families of African ancestry. The Afrigeneas Web site (Fig. 6-11) is associated with the mailing list. The site gathers and presents information

Figure 6-11
The Afrigeneas
Web site.

about families of African ancestry, as well as pointers to genealogical resources around the world. Members of the mailing list are invited to contribute information and resources, perhaps going as far as taking responsibility for information for a certain area.

Generally, when a Web site supplies an About or FAQ (Frequently Asked Questions) page, that's the place to start learning about the site. And Afrigeneas is no exception. Afrigeneas FAQ (http://www.msstate.edu/ Archives/History/afrigen/faq.html) gives you background information on the mailing list that this site is an extension of.

Next, check out the latest edition of AfriGeneas News (http:// members.aol.com/gfsclint/Afrigeneas_News4.html), a monthly newsletter, as well as the Selected AFRIGENEAS Messages link (http://www.afrinet .net/~hallh/afrogene/talk/). This will give you a feel for the community this Web site serves. Now you should be ready to start making use of the resources available at Afrigeneas.

One of the valuable tools you'll find here is the AfriGeneas Database (http://members.aol.com/afriamgene/surnames/sig-name.html) (Fig. 6-12). This database is a collection of surnames of people of African ancestry.

■■■ ■■■ ■■■ ■■■

Figure 6-12
The AfriGeneas Database is a database of surnames for people of African ancestry.

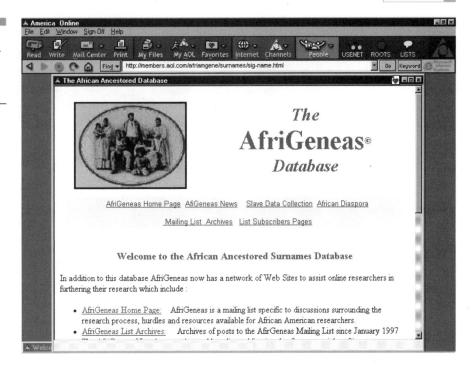

What's most interesting about this database is that it isn't really a database of genealogical information. Instead, it is a database of contacts.

To use the database, you click on the first letter of the surname you are interested in. This takes you to a list of surnames that begin with that letter. Now click on a particular surname. You don't get a collection of genealogical information about that surname. Instead, you see the AOL Compose Mail window. On the To: line of that window, the AfriGeneas Database inserts the e-mail address of the person who has information about the surname you clicked. You can then enter the surname in question on the Subject: line and send a message directly to a person who can help you find information about that surname. This person-to-person approach helps to build connections among researchers, and fits well with the philosophy "Each One Teach One" that is stated in the Afrigeneas FAQ

The African American Information section of the Afrigeneas home page is worth a look too. The links here lead into the Historical Text Archive at Mississippi State University, the school that hosts the Afrigeneas Web site and mailing list. Links such as Black Craftsmen in North Carolina, and Happy Hill, Winston Salem, NC may have exactly the infor-

mation you need. If not, these pages have links directly into the Historical Text Archive (http://www.msstate.edu/Archives/History/index.html),
where you can find plenty of original sources in the African American
History area.

The Afrigeneas Web site also provides plenty of links to other genealogy resources on the Web and Net, oriented both toward general genealogy and genealogy of people of African ancestry. Two of the links we
found particularly interesting are:

- **National Park Service Database on African American Soldiers
  in the Civil War** (http://www.itd.nps.gov/cwss/usct.html) (Fig. 6-13),
  which contains the names of over 230,000 people who served in the
  United States Colored Troops during the war.

- **Slave Data Collection Page** is an FTP site at AOL with the birth,
  death, and ownership records for slaves throughout the 1700s and 1800s.

Tracking Your Roots (http://members.aol.com/ GenWebLisa/)

The Tennessee River, which flows through North Alabama, was a major
westward migration route from Tennessee, Virginia, and the Carolinas. If

Figure 6-13
This database of
information about
African American
soldiers who fought
in the Civil War is only
one of the useful links
from the Afrigeneas
Web site.

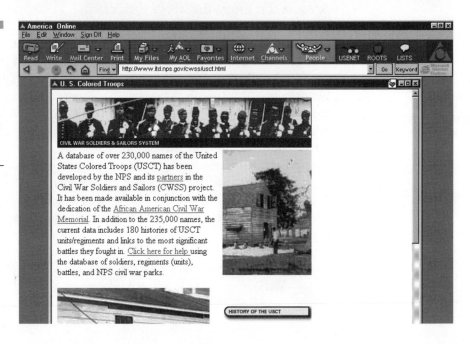

any of your ancestors went west, there is a reasonable chance they followed the Tennessee and passed through Alabama. If so, you may find them in the information you can reach from this site (Fig. 6-14).

If you live in Alabama and have a family reunion planned, you can put out the word by posting information on Tracking Your Roots. Who knows, maybe a long-lost relative will spot the information and appear at the reunion. Contact Lisa R. Franklin, R.N. for more information. She is the person who maintains this fine site—and also a fellow AOL member!

The meatiest part of this site comes next. Click **Tracking Your Alabama Roots: Online Data at Tracking Your Roots** (http://members .aol.com/GenWebLisa/tyralachart.htm) and you'll find an incredible collection of genealogical data (see Fig. 6-15). The material here is listed by county, with additional sections for military as well as statewide and miscellaneous information.

For each county listed, there is at least one link, with most counties having anywhere from 4 to 40 or more links. To give you an idea of the kinds of information you can find here, we've listed the names of some of the different links you'll find on this page:

Figure 6-14
If one of your ancestors went west, they may have traveled the Tennessee river for part of their trip. You should look for them on this site.

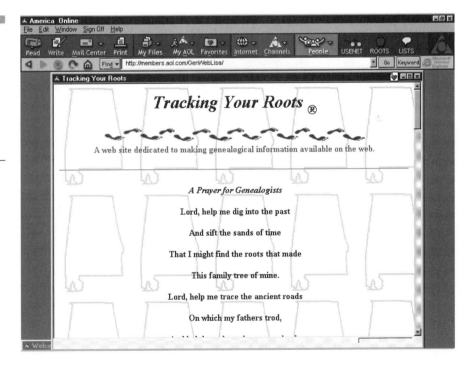

Figure 6-15
Government information useful to genealogists, organized county by county.

- The *Anniston Star* Obituaries
- 1810 Census: Baldwin County, Mississippi Territory
- 1855 State Census of Tallapoosa County, AL
- 1860 Walker County, AL Mortality Schedule
- AL 29th Infantry Co., CSA (Confederate States of America)
- Alabama Bible Records
- Alabama Divorces: 1818–1830
- Alabama Genealogical Societies, Libraries, and Research Sources
- Bullock County, Alabama Cemeteries
- Escambia Co., AL Birth Registers
- Jefferson County, Alabama Marriages: 1818–1859
- Poll Tax Cards: Covington County, Alabama
- Taxable Property in Madison Co., MS Territory—Dated 19 JUL 1810
- War Records of Clarke County Veterans

While most of these resources are found elsewhere on the Net, the fact that they can all be reached from links at Tracking Your Roots is pretty impressive all by itself.

An important link that takes you off Tracking Your Roots to another AOL Web page is Cindy's Southern Genealogy (http://members.aol.com/CindyJ4/index.html), a site that links information from many southern states (Fig. 6-16).

Cindy's site covers a much wider area than Tracking Your Roots, but doesn't include nearly as many links for each locale. You can find information for Alabama, Arkansas, Florida, Georgia, Kentucky, Louisiana, Mississippi, North Carolina, South Carolina, Tennessee, Texas, West Virginia, and Virginia.

USGenWeb (http://www.usgenweb.org/)

The USGenWeb Project is a group of volunteers working to provide non-commercial genealogy Web sites in every county of every state in the

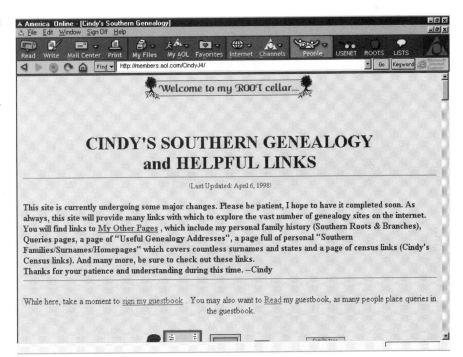

Figure 6-16

Expand your research in the South by visiting Cindy's Southern Genealogy.

United States. These sites are freely accessible to anyone—no memberships or fees required. The online center of this effort is the USGenWeb Project Home Page at http://www.usgenweb.org (Fig. 6-17).

Originally, GENWEB was a single entry point for all counties in Kentucky, where collected databases would be stored. In addition, the databases would be indexed and cross-linked, so even if an individual were found in more than one county, he or she could be located in the index. The idea quickly caught on and has been taken far beyond Kentucky. Today (mid-1998) there are links to every state, plus the District of Columbia. Each state site is unique, with its own look and feel. The state level sites serve as your gateways to the counties within the states. State sites are also the best place for certain activities, like unknown county queries, family reunion bulletins, state history, and county maps. Some state sites are working on special projects such as transcribing Civil War troop records or reuniting families.

You'll see lots of variety at the county level. Every page or database is created by a volunteer, and the resources they provide can be as individualistic as the people themselves. But at a minimum, each county site pro-

Figure 6-17
The USGenWeb Project Home Page is the place to start for county by county genealogical information.

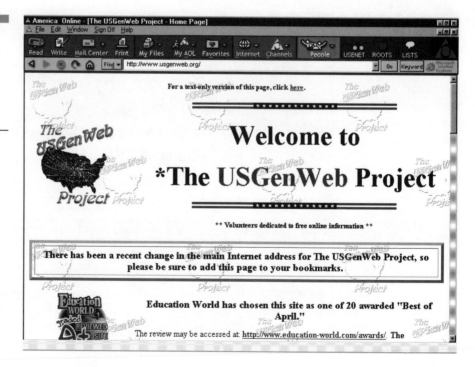

vides links to post queries, get back to the state's home page, and access state archives. USGenWeb is an impressive accomplishment, and the volunteers who do the work deserve the thanks of everyone doing genealogical research in the United States.

━ ━ ━ ━ ━ ━ ━ ━ ━ ━ ━ ━ ━ ━ ━ ━ ━ ━ ━ ━

NOTE   *If you have a lot of genealogical information about a particular county, check the listing on that county in the USGenWeb Project. Maybe you should join the volunteers who make this project possible. If you're interested, click the Information for Current and Prospective Volunteers link. This takes you to the Volunteers page (http://www.usgenweb.org/volunteers/volunteers.html), where you can learn about being a volunteer.*

While the main objective for USGenWeb is the creation of the county-by-county sites, there are also several special projects under way. You can find out about them on the USGenWeb Special Projects page (http://www.usgenweb.org/projects/projects.html). Some of the special projects under way at this writing are:

■ *Archives Project.*   USGenWeb was originally designed to provide information county by county, but there is plenty of genealogical information that can't be organized this way. The Archive Project aims to put noncounty public domain information onto the Web. This project has several subprojects, including the Tombstone Project (http://www.rootsweb.com/~cemetery/) shown in Fig. 6-18. In this subproject, volunteers are traveling to cemeteries around the country and transcribing the inscriptions on the tombstones. These inscriptions are then made accessible through this Web page.

■ *Lineage Project.*   For people who want track down a particular ancestor, this project provides a place to list information about the ancestor and contact information (an e-mail address or Web page) for the researcher.

■ *National and International Links Project.*   This is a collection of links from USGenWeb to sites of general genealogical interest around the world.

Going back to the USGenWeb home page, another link you should check out is Information for Researchers (http://www.usgenweb.org/researchers/researcher.html). This takes you to a page full of helpful research tips, plus an interesting section on taking care of old documents. As a genealogist, you probably have some old books, photos, and news-

Figure 6-18
The Tombstone
Project is just one
piece of USGenWeb's
Archive Project.

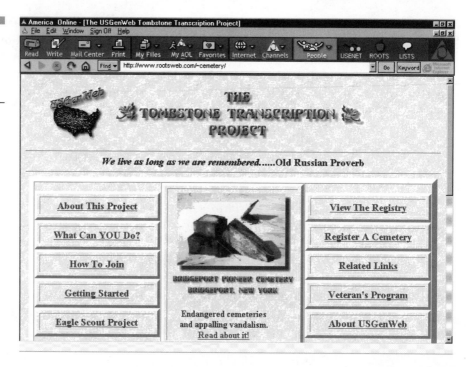

Figure 6-18
The Tombstone
Project is just one
piece of USGenWeb's
Archive Project.

paper articles you would like to preserve. Visit the Information for Researchers page and learn how to preserve these precious pieces of family history.

After these highlights of the USGenWeb Project Home Page, we're sure you'll agree that this is an important destination if you are researching roots within the United States.

Library of Congress (http://www.loc.gov/)

The mission of the Library of Congress is to "make its resources available and useful to the Congress and the American people and to sustain and preserve a universal collection of knowledge and creativity for future generations." To that end, the Library of Congress has, since its founding in 1800, amassed more than 100 million items, and has become one of the world's leading cultural institutions. The Library of Congress Web site (Fig. 6-19) makes a small portion of the Library's contents available to the world through the Internet.

Figure 6-19
The Library of
Congress Web site
is a vast general
information source
with some significant
genealogical
resources.

Three sections of the Web site are of particular use to genealogists. The American Memory section contains documents, photographs, movies, and sound recordings that tell some of America's story. The Research Tools section of the site offers many online databases and connections to resources at other sites. The American Treasures section of the site is of interest more for the wonderful historical artifacts found there than for any specific genealogy information.

Click the American Memory link to begin your exploration of the Library of Congress site. The subtitle for this page is "Historical Collections for the National Digital Library." This project is a public-private partnership that is designed to create a digital library of reproductions of primary source material that will support research into the history and culture of the United States of America. Since this is an ongoing project, you can expect that the resources here will continue to grow for the foreseeable future.

If you are researching African American roots, you'll want to click the African American Odyssey link. This exhibition examines the African American quest for full citizenship, and contains primary source material as well as links to other African American materials at the Library.

Going back to the American Memory Home Page, you can click **Documents** to explore other primary source material. Some of the items you'll find here include:

- Almost 200 books describing the personal experiences of individuals in and on the way to California during and after the gold rush.
- Hundreds of objects dealing with the Women's Suffrage movement.
- Significant and interesting documents from Americans obscure to famous, as collected in the first 100 years of the Library of Congress Manuscript Division.
- American Life Histories: Manuscripts from the Federal Writer's Project, 1936–1940.

A third area of the American Memory section of the Library for you to explore is the Maps section. Clicking **Maps** brings you to a searchable Web page (http://memory.loc.gov/ammem/mapcoll23.html) containing hundreds of digitized maps from 1639 to 1988. You'll find city maps, conservation maps, exploration maps, immigration and settlement maps, military maps, and transportation maps, to name a few. And the amazing thing is that this wealth of maps is only a tiny part of the Library of Congress's full 4.5-million-item Geography and Map Division holdings.

The Research Tools link from the Library of Congress Home Page takes you to a large set of useful databases, as well as links to other resources of interest for researchers. One such link is Vietnam Era Prisoner of War/ Missing in Action and Task Force Russia Databases (http://lcweb2.loc.gov/ pow/powhome.html). This takes you to a page (Fig. 6-20) that gives you access to a massive database of over 137,000 records pertaining to U.S. military personnel listed as unaccounted for as of December 1991.

At the bottom of this page is a link to Task Force Russia (http://lcweb2 .loc.gov/frd/tfrquery.html), a set of documents dealing with Americans who are believed to have been held in the former Soviet Union.

Finally, under the Exhibitions heading on the Library of Congress Home Page, check out the American Treasures of the Library of Congress link. You'll find reproductions of dozens of the most treasured objects in the Library's collection. Each one of the objects featured, from the *Whole Booke of Psalmes Faithfully Translated into English Metre* (1640), to the Dorothea Lange notebooks shown in Fig. 6-21, to a Game Program for the Kansas City Monarchs vs. Indianapolis Clowns (1954) has some special historical significance. You may not find any long-lost ancestors when browsing this collection, but there's sure to be something of interest to every genealogist.

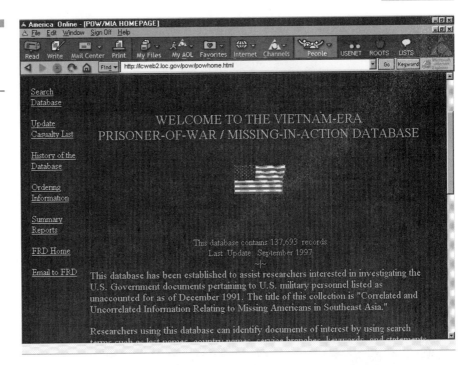

Figure 6-20
POWs and MIAs from the Vietnam War era are recorded here.

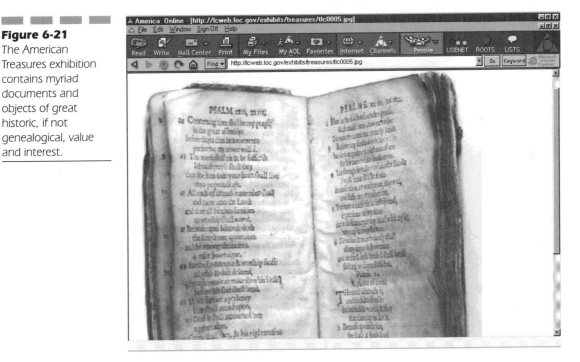

Figure 6-21
The American Treasures exhibition contains myriad documents and objects of great historic, if not genealogical, value and interest.

Find Your Own Favorites

The World Wide Web is a big place, and finding exactly the resources that you want can be difficult. People quickly realized that what the Web needed was an index. Or two. Or five. You can now find more than 15 major sites that serve as guides to what's on the World Wide Web and the Internet in general. And they're all free.

Start with America Online's AOL NetFind (Keyword: *NETFIND*). In AOL 4.0, you can click on **Find** on the Tool Bar and choose **Find on the Web**.

For information on NetFind and other tools for finding what you want on the Web, go to Chap. 7. But first, consider another way to be sure you can always find the genealogical resources you want on the Web: creating your own genealogy Web site. It's easy, thanks to AOL. Doing this is the topic of the last section of this chapter.

Publishing Your Own Genealogy Web Page with AOL Personal Publisher

There are many tools available for creating your own page on the World Wide Web. Some of these tools are expensive or difficult to use. As an America Online subscriber, you don't need to worry about tools. All AOL subscribers have access to Personal Publisher, an easy-to-use and free (aside from the usual connect charges) Web page creation tool. The templates provided by the program make it easy to create several types of Web pages, including a personal home page, a business home page, or a greeting card. You can also use Personal Publisher to directly create custom Web pages. And you don't even have to know HTML, the language of the World Wide Web. If you do know HTML, you have even more design options.

Once you create your Web pages, you can easily upload them to My Place, the area on the AOL reserves for each member's Web pages. (Each account gets 10 megabytes of storage). Once your pages are uploaded to My Place, other AOL subscribers, or anyone with a Web browser anywhere on the Internet, can see your pages. It's that simple.

To get started, go to Keyword: *Personal Publisher* (Fig. 6-22).

Figure 6-22

Personal Publisher is the easy way to create your own genealogy Web page.

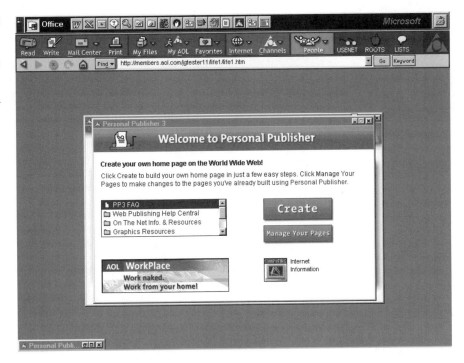

NOTE   *At the time of this writing, AOL was revising Personal Publisher to greatly improve and enhance this valuable tool. The instructions here are taken from the beta version of Personal Publisher 3. Look for many more templates and online communities in the near future.*

The first step in using Personal Publisher to create your own genealogy Web page is the same as for any new site you might find on the Web: read the About and Frequently Asked Question files. These files have the background information you need to get going.

Once you've finished reading the About and FAQ files, you're almost ready to start Personal Publisher. But before you do, think about your Web page. Do you want to build a personal genealogy page, one that carries your family information? Do you want to build an index to the genealogy sites you think are most useful? Before you start designing your page or pages, make sure you know why you are doing this.

Assuming you've spent some time thinking about what you want to do on the Web, it is time to start designing your home page. Start by clicking **Create** in the Personal Publisher window. Personal Publisher offers several templates (ideal if you haven't ever designed a Web page before), as well as a **Blank Page** option. For your first try, we recommend the Personal template. Click the template to get started.

Personal Publisher begins by asking you to enter a title and greeting for your page. You can now see why Personal Publisher makes it so easy to build your Web pages. It works similarly to a Wizard in Microsoft Windows—just answer the questions in each window and let Personal Publisher build the page for you. Click **Next** to go on to the next window. Click **Cancel** to stop designing your Web page. Click **?** to get context-sensitive help (help that's specific to the window you are working on).

After choosing a title and headline, you get to select a background and text color for your page. After the background and text color, it's time to choose an image that will appear on your page. Here you can choose from the images provided by the program, or browse the files on your computer for that perfect image. And on it goes, with Personal Publisher guiding you through all the options.

Once you've worked through all the steps to create your page, a window lets you preview your creation (Fig. 6-23). You can choose **Publish** if

Figure 6-23
With a basic Web page built, it's time for some fine-tuning before publishing the page to the World Wide Web.

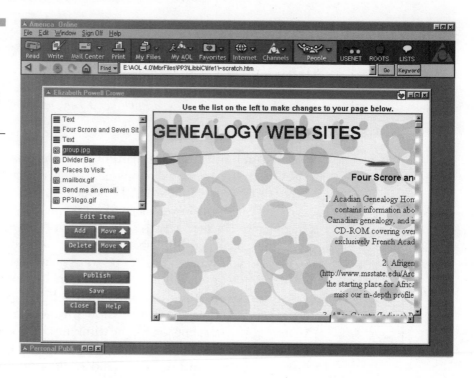

you are happy with it, or choose **Edit**. This returns you to the main PP page, where you can click on **Manage Your Pages** to get the editor.

Here you can do several things:

- There is a list of the elements of your page (pictures, text, title, etc.) in a scroll-down box. Highlight any one element at a time and click **Edit Item** to change things on your page, or you can add your own HTML code to the page to do things Personal Publisher doesn't automatically do for you. HTML isn't really that hard to learn, and you should consider doing so if you are serious about your Web pages.

- You can Publish your Web page. This uploads it to My Place, which is an area on the America Online servers reserved for your screen name. Once you upload your Web page, anyone subscribing to AOL, as well as anyone with a Web browser and an Internet connection, can view your page.

- Click one of the **Move** buttons to rearrange the items.

- Click **HELP** to get help on any of the options.

Once you finish editing your page, it's time to publish it. Just follow these steps:

1. Click **Publish**, then sit back and wait a moment. Personal Publisher will take care of uploading the page, using the title and file name you gave it in the beginning of the process.

2. Click **Ok**, and Personal Publisher transfers your page to My Place.

3. Personal Publisher shows you the URL (address) of your new Web page and asks if you want it added to your Favorite Places list. Click **Yes** or **No**.

That's the end of the process. Your new page is now on the Web for all to see. Figure 6-24 shows what the example page we put together looks like.

When you want to make changes, simply come back to Keyword: *Personal Publisher*, click on **Manage Pages** and you can add and delete pages. Update your pages often; static sites don't draw eyeballs!

NOTE   *The pages you create with Personal Publisher are stored on a Web server called members.aol.com. This is where My Place for your screen name resides.*

Figure 6-24

The example page is now on the World Wide Web for all to see.

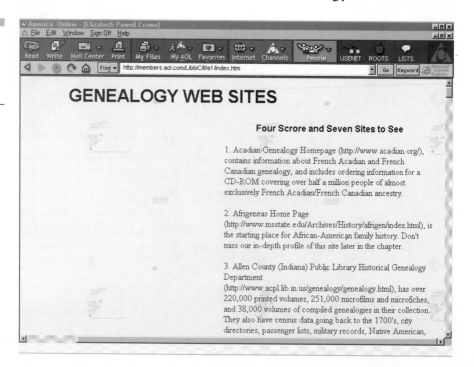

NOTE *Personal Publisher won't keep you from uploading a new file with the same name as one you've already uploaded. If that happens, the new file replaces the old one, and the old one is gone forever.*

CHAPTER 7

AOL NetFind and Other Search Tools

Throughout this book, we've tried to point you to the best genealogy newsgroups and Web sites. But the rate of change on the Internet is incredible. America Online must pick and choose which newsgroups they will carry. Web sites disappear or move to a new server, which changes their URLs. And great new newsgroups and Web sites pop up all the time. Besides, as a genealogist, you know the thrill of discovering things for yourself. It can be quite a kick to find a Web site or newsgroup that none of your friends know about.

So what you need is a way to find genealogical resources on the Internet on your own. You could use sites that link to other sites. But a better way is to search for what you want yourself. That's where search engines and directories come in.

A *search engine* is a program that looks for information on the Internet, creates a database of what it finds, and lets you use a Web browser to search that database for specific information. AOL NetFind (Keyword: *NetFind*) is a powerful search engine that America Online makes available for free to the Internet community and AOL members.

A *directory* is similar to a search engine in that you can search the directory for specific information. But in a directory, the newsgroups and Web sites are sorted, categorized, and sometimes rated. Yahoo! (http://www .yahoo.com) is one example.

The following two sections describe various search engines and directories. While the content in them overlaps a great deal, each one uses slightly different methods to search and rates sites slightly differently. This means you may find what you are looking for with one search engine or directory but not another. In any case, the best place to start a genealogy search is with AOL NetFind.

AOL NetFind

AOL NetFind (http://www.aol.com/netfind/home.html) is a powerful general-purpose search engine with some additional capabilities that are covered elsewhere in this chapter. To reach AOL NetFind from within America Online, you can go to the Internet window and click the **NetFind** button, or you can go directly there by entering Keyword: *NetFind*. In either case, you'll get to the AOL NetFind home page shown in Fig. 7-1.

Figure 7-1
The AOL NetFind
home page is the
place to start when
you want to search
the World Wide Web.

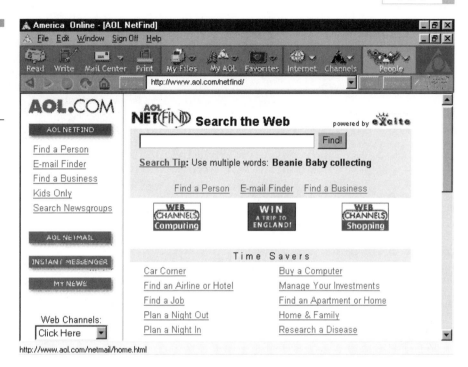

http://www.aol.com/netmail/home.html

To do a basic search, all you have to do is enter the word or phrase you want to search for in the text box and click **Find**! However, in most cases, you'll end up finding too much stuff. For example, a search on the word *genealogy* returned more than 95,000 matches! This is a general problem with search engines, which have been known to return over a million matches for common terms.

To get around this challenge, search engines give you various ways to narrow your searches. Here are some search tips for AOL NetFind.

■ *Use phrases instead of single words in your searches.*   Type several words that are relevant to your search. *Spencer genealogy Ohio* will narrow a search well.

■ *Enclose phrases in quotes.*   Searching with the phrase *Mann family history* will match all pages that have any of those three words included somewhere on the page, in any order, and not necessarily adjacent. Searching with the phrase "*Mann family history*" will return only those pages that have those three words together, in exactly that order.

- *The more specific you are the better.*   Searching for *Irish genealogy databases* will give you fewer, but closer, matches than searching for *Irish genealogy.*

- *Use + and – in your searches.*   A word preceded by a plus sign (+) must appear on the page for there to be a match. A word preceded by a minus sign (–) must not appear on the page for there to be a match. There can be no spaces between the plus or minus signs and the words they apply to. For example, entering "+cats –dogs monkeys" would tell AOL NetFind you wanted pages that definitely used the word *cats,* didn't use the word *dogs,* with *monkeys* optional.

- *Narrow your searches if you get too many matches.*   Once AOL Net Find completes a search, you have the chance to narrow or broaden the search. You do this by going to the **Search** box at the end of the search results page and entering more search terms if you want to narrow the search and removing search terms if you want to broaden the search.

NOTE   *If you want more search tips, click* **Search Tips***. If you are really stuck, follow the links from that page to some advanced tips.*

You now have the basic know-how to use AOL NetFind. Begin your search here, but if you can't find what you want, try another search engine. Some good choices are listed next.

Lycos Web Search (http://www.lycos.com/) works very much like AOL NetFind but may return different results for the same search. Lycos does have some special plusses. The search engine includes separate databases for pictures, sounds, programs, and other categories of information. Lycos is also the home of the Lycos Top 5% (http://point.lycos.com/categories/), a guide to what Lycos feels are the best 5% of all Web sites.

Since Lycos reviewers have to hear of a site, visit it, review it, and post it (assuming the site makes the top 5%) this isn't a good place to look for a brand new site. But if you are looking for sites that someone else has reviewed and rated for you, this is a great resource.

Webcrawler (http://www.webcrawler.com) is another Web search engine. In general, it is not as complete or as fast as the others are. Use it as a last resort.

General Directories

Yahoo! (http://www.yahoo.com) is an edited, sorted catalog of sites. And it is big. It features about half a million sites divided into 25,000 categories. Yahoo! is arranged in a hierarchy of categories, so you can browse through it. But with so many sites and categories, it is good to know that Yahoo! has a search engine built in. Mind you, this search engine doesn't search the Web, it searches Yahoo! looking for sites and categories within the directory.

Yahoo! gets updated frequently, with users providing most of the new sites. Each site gets visited by a Yahoo! surfer, who decides where each site should appear within the directory.

InfoSeek (http://www.infoseek.com/) is an Internet directory similar to Yahoo! You can browse the InfoSeek (Fig. 7-2) channels (categories), or you can run a search on the contents of the InfoSeek databases. When doing searches on InfoSeek, capitalization counts, so you can search for surnames such as Weeks and Fox without getting as many irrelevant matches. Like AOL NetFind, InfoSeek uses plus and minus signs in its

Figure 7-2
InfoSeek is another massive directory you can use.

searches. In addition, InfoSeek doesn't ignore common words like *the* and *new,* so you can efficiently search for states like New Hampshire.

As you can see in Fig. 7-2, some Internet directories and search engines are branching out from their roots to offer services like stock reports and news, even UPS package tracking. InfoSeek is trying to become a comprehensive source of online information. Time will tell whether this works out or not.

People Search Engines

So far, you've looked at the search engines and directories for finding a Web site. But what if you need to find lost, living relatives? In that case, you need people search engines. These specialize in finding people, not pages. As with regular search engines, the place to start is at the versatile AOL NetFind.

AOL NetFind (http://www.aol.com/netfind/person.html) and (http://www.aol.com/netfind/emailfinder.html) actually has two sections that can help you find people. The first (Fig. 7-3) is the Find a Person page. Here you can enter the first and last names of a person as well as the city (optional) and state the person lives in. A successful search turns up a person's mailing address and phone number. Beside each name returned by the search are three buttons. You can send them personal greetings, flowers, or some other gift.

NOTE   *The people you find using the Find a Person window are U.S. Residents.*

The E-mail Finder lets you find the e-mail address of a person if you know their first and last names.

Four11 (www.four11.com) is one of many White Pages services on the Web. It's free and has the e-mail and telephone numbers of millions of people and businesses taken from public records, as well as a Web site catalog. If you register as a user (it's free), you can ensure that your listing is not only accurate but also has only the information you wish it to reveal.

Figure 7-3

Tracking down people is easy with the Find a Person feature.

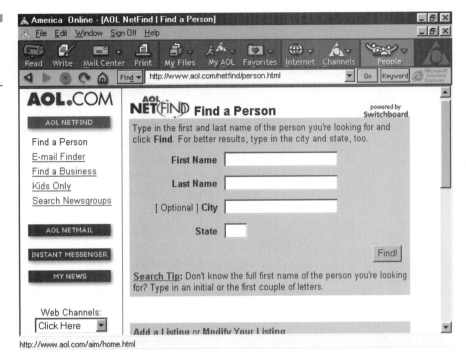

BigFoot (http://www.bigfoot.com) is another such effort to catalog people, with the same general rules: input your information and you get searches that are more specific. BigFoot also has surface mail addresses as well as e-mail and telephone information.

File Search Sites

Sometimes what the online genealogist needs isn't a site or a person—it's a program. To find programs you may hear of, such as new Web browsers or genealogy programs, you can go to several sites that keep track of software and where the latest versions are. Some of these are AOL's Software Center, File Mine, TUCOWS, Shareware.com, and ZDNet Software Library.

Start with AOL's Software Center (Keyword: *FIND SOFTWARE*). Here you have four choices: search for shareware (try-before-you-buy programs such as Brother's Keeper); search for commercial software (such as Family Tree Maker); check out the recommended Daily Download (usually a general purpose program); or investigate the Computing Superstore.

To search for shareware, click the link. You'll get the Software Search window (Keyword: *FILESEARCH*). You can limit your search by time (All dates, Past month, Past week) in which the file was uploaded and by categories: applications, operating system, and so on. Then type your keywords (*genealogy programs*, for example). In a few seconds you have a list of matches. You can select one, read its description, and decide whether to add it to your Download Manager list of files to be downloaded. When you have your list complete, you can just choose Download Manager from the window that pops up when you choose Download Later and tell it to start.

File Mine (http://www.filemine.com) is a vast collection of software, most uploaded by the authors and offered as shareware, or rarely, freeware. File Mine catalogs and rates the software. In the category Home & Leisure, you'll find a Genealogy section, but as of this writing, it was empty. However, you can search the database, and *genealogy* comes up with such all-time favorites as Brother's Keeper and Family Matters. When you find a category that has files in it, you can choose to look at their edited catalogs of software. Under Jewels, you'll find software judged best in its class. Under Packs, you'll find customized collections of software around a theme (holidays, privacy, etc.). Digs, on the other hand, gives you a list of software that competes head to head (Web browsers, etc.). New will have the newest files.

The Ultimate Collection of Winsock Software, TUCOWS (http://www.tucows.com), is a site that tracks more than Windows, despite the name, and has a capsule profile and a rating for each program. TUCOWS has mirror sites all over the world, so you can choose a site close to you for faster downloads.

Shareware.com (http://www.shareware.com) is a premier software search site. Updated weekly, the search engine lets you choose your operating system, choose a keyword and even choose a date for the newest software *or* the oldest! Shareware.com then lets you see where the file can be found and rates the reliability (how easy it is to get in and get a file) of each site.

ZDNet Software Library (http://www.hotfiles.com/) has the latest software, usually rated by the staff on a five-star system. All the ZD sites are

Figure 7-4

If you want to download a program, AOL's software search area.

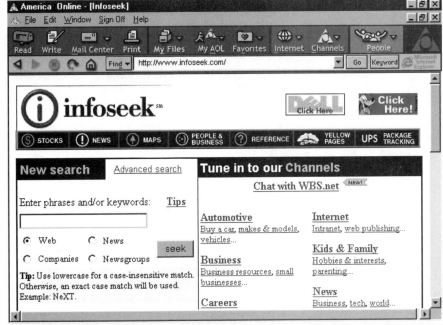

now integrated to some extent, so you can search from the ZDNet Software Library into a bunch of magazines (*PC Magazine, Computer Shopper,* and *Yahoo! Internet Life,* to name a few) for site reviews as well as the latest software.

Searching for Information Within Newsgroups

While newsgroups can be great sources of genealogy information, reading all the messages, or even the headers, can be a lot of work. Fortunately, you don't always have to read the whole newsgroup to find the information you need. There are several places where you can search newsgroups, one or several, or all at a time. As an America Online user, the logical place for you to start is our old friend AOL NetFind.

AOL NetFind's Search Newsgroups page (Fig. 7-5) lets you search either the messages in newsgroups (called articles in AOL NetFind) or the newsgroup descriptions.

Like the other sections of AOL NetFind, the Search Newsgroups window has an area for you to enter search terms. The search tips for newsgroups are different than those for Web sites, so if you are having trouble finding what you are looking for, your best bet is to click the **Newsgroup Search Tips** link and get tips specifically for this search engine.

In addition to the newsgroup search engine, the Search Newsgroups page includes a good-sized directory of newsgroups (the Newsgroup Scoop section) divided into categories like travel, shopping, and international. Try the Families and Local links to find genealogy-related newsgroups.

The search engine for InfoSeek (http://www.infoseek.com) can not only search Web sites but also newsgroups, news archives, and company listings as well. With regard to newsgroups, InfoSeek has the most recent two weeks of newsgroups stored in a searchable database. To search newsgroups, just enter the text you want to search for, click **Newsgroups**, then

Figure 7-5

This section of AOL NetFind lets you search newsgroups.

Figure 7-6
Deja News carries two
and one-half years'
worth of newsgroup
messages.

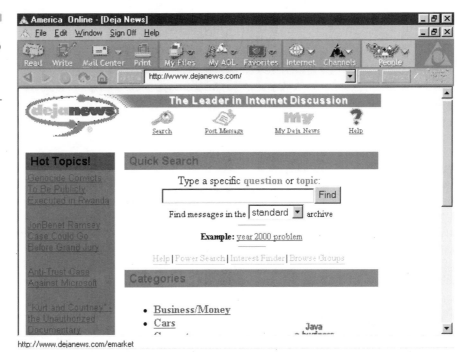

http://www.dejanews.com/emarket

click **seek**. To do quick and easy genealogical searches, type in the surnames you are interested in and follow them with *+genealogy*. InfoSeek will return a list of the genealogical messages. Each message title is a link; click on it to read it.

The people at Deja News (http://www.dejanews.com) created the search engine that powers the Search Newsgroups page at AOL NetFind. So it's no wonder that we find Deja News (Fig. 7-6) is a favorite tool of ours.

Deja News carries over 50,000 newsgroups, with postings going back as far as two and one-half years, and it makes basic searches simple, yet supports more complex ones. You can click **Power Search** to get fancy. Create a Query Filter by typing in the first part of the name of a group of newsgroups you want to search. For example, enter soc.genealogy.*. Now type in the surnames you're looking for and click **find**. Within seconds, Deja News will return a list of messages that are in the soc.genealogy.* groups and mention the surnames you gave it.

PART

4

Other Genealogical Resources

America Online and Internet services like mailing lists or the Web aren't the only online genealogy resources you can tap. The chapters in this part cover two other online resources that may be useful in your research.

- Online card catalogs let you save time and effort by searching for the library books you need without ever leaving home.

- The Mormon Church has the most extensive computerized repository of genealogical data on earth. While it isn't accessible through AOL or the Web (at least not yet), you can get access to this data if you know how.

CHAPTER **8**

Online Library Card Catalogs

Despite all the wonderful things appearing online, many of your genealogical expeditions will still be in libraries. But you can use AOL to search some libraries, too.

One of the wonderful things about the online world is the plethora of libraries going to electronic card catalogs. Of course, this speeds up the search when you are physically present in the library. With an online catalog and many terminals scattered throughout the building, you don't have to look up your subject, author, or title on one floor, then run to another to actually find the referenced material. If your local library hasn't computerized its card catalog yet, it probably will soon.

But oh, the joys of looking in the card catalog before you actually visit the library. You know immediately whether that library owns the title. With a few more keystrokes, you can find out whether the title is on the shelf, on reserve, on loan to someone, or lost without a trace. If the title in question isn't at that library or branch, you can find out whether the book is available by interlibrary loan. Some libraries are part of an online system, like the Greater Manchester Integrated Library Cooperative System (Fig. 8-1). These systems link groups of libraries, allowing you to

Figure 8-1

Sometimes a group of libraries shares a Web site, making it easy to search all of them at once.

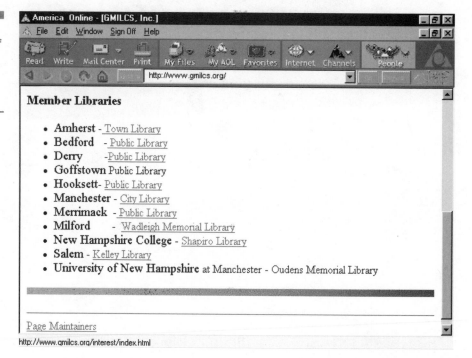

Member Libraries

- **Amherst** - Town Library
- **Bedford** - Public Library
- **Derry** - Public Library
- **Goffstown** Public Library
- **Hooksett** - Public Library
- **Manchester** - City Library
- **Merrimack** - Public Library
- **Milford** - Wadleigh Memorial Library
- **New Hampshire College** - Shapiro Library
- **Salem** - Kelley Library
- **University of New Hampshire** at Manchester - Oudens Memorial Library

Page Maintainers

http://www.gmilcs.org/interest/index.html

search for titles across most or all of the libraries in the area. Some more advanced systems will even let you enter your library card number, in effect checking the book out to yourself without leaving home.

There are two main ways to connect to online card catalogs. The newest and easiest way is through the World Wide Web. The card catalog appears to be like any of the Web-based databases you've encountered in this book. Or the connection could be by telnet. Here you use a separate program to send commands to, and receive information from, the database. More on this later in the chapter.

A third way to connect to an online card catalog is with a hybrid Web-telnet connection. In this case, the library (or libraries) maintains a Web site with all the relevant information on how to use the card catalog. Then, when it is time to actually look at the card catalog database, the AOL browser starts a telnet program to actually work with the database.

Connecting to Card Catalogs by Web Browser

The easiest and most visually appealing way to connect to online card catalogs is via the World Wide Web. The mechanics of how this works are irrelevant. What's important is that a Web-based interface lets you use the card catalog without having to install and load a telnet program.

A wonderful example is the University of Texas at Austin's UTNetCAT (http://dpweb1.dp.utexas.edu/lib/utnetcat/). You can use the forms that appear at this Web site (Fig. 8-2) to search by author, title, subject, or any combination. The results of the search are links to the card catalog.

Another, slightly more complicated example is at the University of Alabama in Huntsville Web site. By going directly to the complex search page for the card catalog at (http://libsirsi.uah.edu/uhtbin/cgisirsi/33/60/30034), you can choose any of several ways to enter search terms (Fig. 8-3). You can find items that contain certain words or phrases in any field. Using boolean operators (AND, OR), you can specify that words, author names, title words, or subject terms must have a particular relationship to each other. If you want something written by a specific person, searching by Author makes sense. If you know most of the words in the title, a Title search can tell you if the library has the item and where it is located. If you don't know an author or title, you can search by Subject.

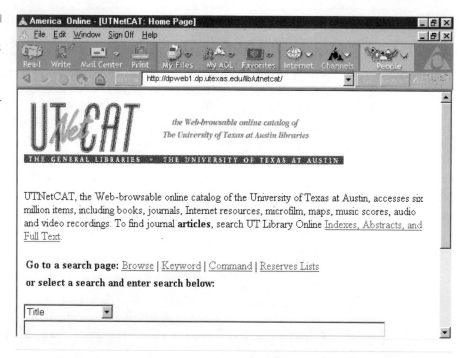

You'll have better luck with your searches if you narrow them as much as possible. Search on Author and Title, Subject, and Word or Phrase. Optionally, you can search recent issues of magazines with the Periodical Title option.

To show you how this works, we chose a search with *genealogy* in the general keyword field and *Alabama* in the subject field. Figure 8-4 shows the results of that search. The search turned up seven cards that matched our search criteria. Each matching card has a short synopsis that appears on the Results page. By clicking the **View** button next to a synopsis, you can get additional details about the card. Do this, and you will see information like the publication date, author, and cross-links to other relevant cards in the catalog. You can print the results, or have a copy of them e-mailed to you.

Another nice Web site to see is the card catalog for the University of Virginia (http://eagle.vsla.edu/catalog/). The wonderful thing about this system is the library's collection of Bible records. Go to the page shown in Fig. 8-5 to test out this system yourself.

We ran a test with *genealogy* as the general keyword, and *Powell* as the subject keyword. The results (see Fig. 8-6) consist of links directly to the

Figure 8-4

The results of a search at this site include a short synopsis.

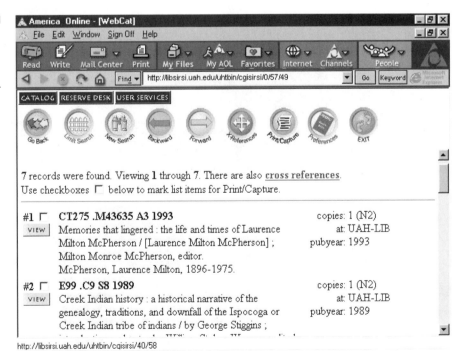

Figure 8-5
The Library of Virginia includes extensive Bible records.

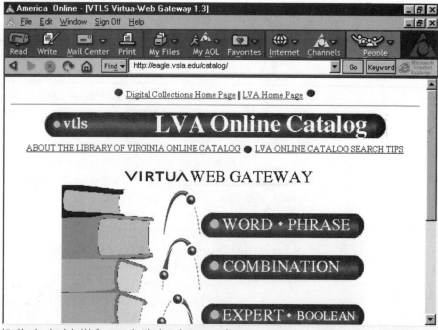

Figure 8-6
The results of a search here are links to the actual cards in the catalog.

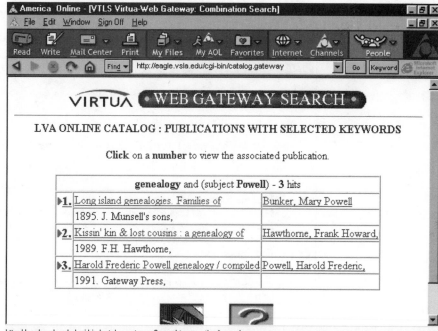

catalog's cards. This card catalog also allows you to use boolean terms (AND, NOT, etc.) to further refine your searches. This card catalog presentation is very easy to understand and read, a real pleasure to work with.

Connecting to Card Catalogs by Telnet

Some card catalogs, while online, haven't been put in Web format. You have to get at them another way. That way is with telnet. Telnet is a system that lets you connect to another computer as if your PC were a terminal on that computer, regardless of where each computer actually is. Telnet is an older Internet service but is still in fairly widespread use for online card catalogs.

Windows 95 comes with a basic telnet program. The version of Internet Explorer that serves as the Web browser for AOL is designed to automatically activate that telnet program whenever it tries to connect to a telnet address. There's no setting up for you to do. Just enter the telnet address on the browser's Address line and a telnet window will pop up, ready to go. For more details, go to Keyword: *TELNET* (see Fig. 8-7).

Figure 8-7
The telnet area on AOL.

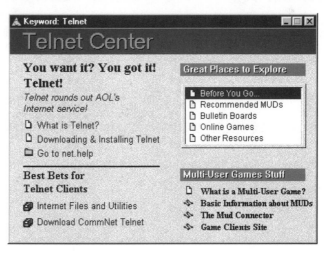

A typical example of an online card catalog you can reach using telnet and the Internet is the South Carolina State Library card catalog (telnet://leo.scsl.state.sc.us). Enter this address, and the Web browser will start the telnet program with a connection to the library. Enter the password (LION) listed in the first window (just type it in where the cursor appears) and press **Enter**. You'll see the library's Main Menu (Fig. 8-8).

We started by typing a *1* (one) to get into the LION card catalog and began our research with a Subject search. We searched for the term *genealogy*, and the catalog returned a list of cards that had the term *genealogy* on them. We also got a number of references to other sections of the card catalog (see Fig. 8-9).

If you've ever used the electronic card catalog at your local library, this should all look pretty familiar to you. By following the on-screen instructions, you can find out what titles are available, where they are located, and, in short, get all the information you would get if you were physically in the library looking at the card catalog.

Figure 8-8
The library's main menu.

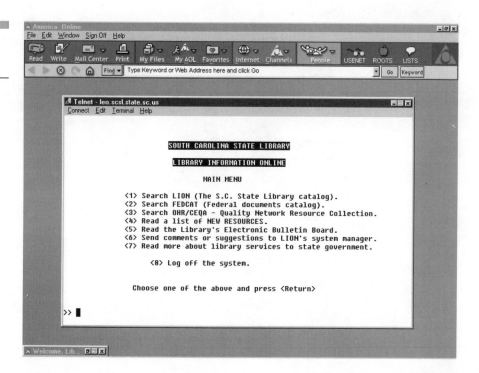

Figure 8-9

The results of a search of the South Carolina State Library card catalog.

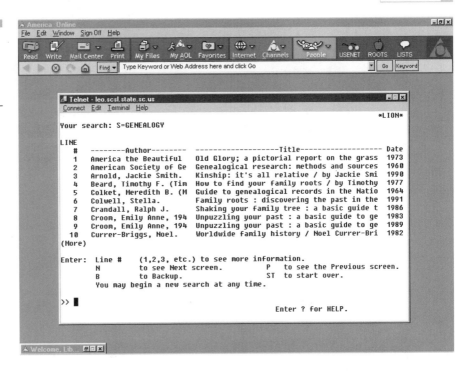

Figure 8-10

Here's a collection of online card catalogs you can use to browse through the Web or telnet.

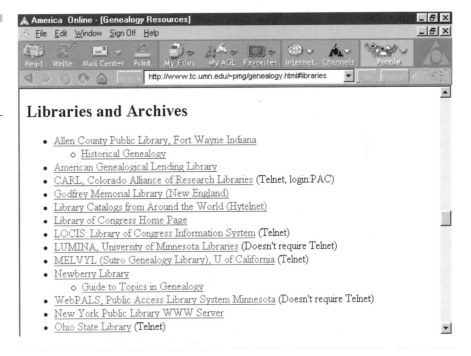

Where to Find More Online Card Catalogs

Once you've explored the online card catalogs shown in this chapter, it's likely you'll want to find some more. One place to look for both the Web and telnet kinds is the Genealogy Resources page at the University of Minnesota. Browse down to the Libraries and Archives section (http://www .tc.umn.edu/~pmg/genealogy.html#libraries). As Fig. 8-10 shows, this section of the page includes links to both types of online card catalogs.

Learn to use these systems. Who knows what treasures you will find!

CHAPTER 9

LDS: The Church of Jesus Christ of Latter-Day Saints

As we've noted before in this book, one of the most frequently asked genealogy questions online is: "Can I connect to Mormon genealogy information with my modem?" The answer is, "No."

So why did we include this chapter? First, because the Church of Jesus Christ of Latter-Day Saints (often abbreviated as LDS) has many computerized resources. While these resources are not currently available online, the church will willingly share the information as a public service through their Family History Centers.

Second, we included this chapter because the genealogical information of the church is slowly becoming available to libraries, archives, societies, and the general public. It's only a matter of time before this material becomes available online somewhere.

Third, you simply cannot talk about modern genealogical research without talking about the Mormons, so it seems natural to include their publicly available resources in this book.

And finally, even if you are not a Mormon, you are bound to find useful data in their records. The genealogies go back beyond the beginning of the Mormon church and include relatives who never became Mormons. There may be a connection to your family somewhere, because as we've said, mathematically we all have to be kin somehow.

Some Background

Without trying to explain the theology involved, we'll simply say that Mormons consider it a religious duty to research their family history. If you want to understand why, you can visit the LDS site on the Web at http://www.lds.org (Fig. 9-1). The specific page with this information is http://www.lds.org/Family_History/Why_Family_History.html.

The results of Mormon genealogical research are archived at the church's headquarters in Salt Lake City, Utah. They're distributed to the many Family History Centers (FHC) around the world by microfilm, microfiche, and CD-ROM. The data is in several forms, but the most important to the online genealogists are the Ancestral File (AF) and the International Genealogical Index (IGI). Both of these are updated frequently. As of this writing, the databases occupied seven highly compressed CD-ROMs.

One of the LDS's objectives is to enlarge their copyrighted AF and IGI databases, while constantly increasing their accuracy and improving the software used to search them.

The AF is a compilation of genealogies contributed by church members and patrons of the Family History Centers alike. The information is

Figure 9-1
The LDS Web site explains much about their beliefs, as well as why Mormons practice genealogy.

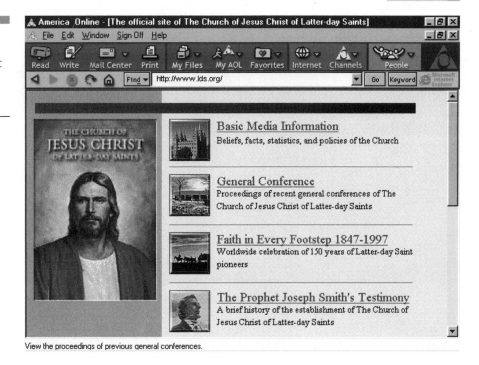

primarily about deceased people and contains millions of names linked into family pedigrees.

The IGI is a record of births, christenings, and marriages for millions of people who lived from the early 1500s to the early 1900s. The data have been extracted from thousands of original church records.

The AF and the IGI are unrelated; data that appears in the AF may not appear in the IGI, and vice versa. Each file has value, and each is worth searching. The biggest advantage of the AF is that you can extract family pedigrees from it. The biggest advantage of the IGI is that it contains more detailed information than the AF.

Most non-LDS genealogists consider the IGI to be the more valuable of the two files. While both files contain errors, the IGI is closer to the original records (Mormon data is normally entered into the IGI first). The IGI offers some excellent bits of information, particularly its references to original source materials.

While many non-LDS genealogists prefer to start with the IGI, the AF (with the new GEDCOM 5.5 format) allows you to find out what documentation supports the entries. In addition to pedigree or descendancy charts, the AF can give you the name and address of the person who submitted the information. It is best not to overlook either of these files.

Although the AF and IGI both have errors, the error rate appears to be low. Plenty of the genealogy books printed in the last 100 years have higher error rates. The fact that this information is compiled and computerized by a religious group in no way compromises its quality.

You should treat the AF and the IGI the same way you would treat a printed book about a surname—with great caution. The information you find in these files gives you excellent clues, but you should always cross-check what you find against primary records. While the computer increases the amount of data you can scan and makes things much easier, it doesn't necessarily improve accuracy. After all, human beings are still the source of all this information.

The LDS apparently wants to make their AF and IGI files available to more people. Originally you had to visit the Family History Center in Salt Lake City to use these databases. Now the CD-ROMs containing this information are on a network that connects to the Joseph Smith Memorial Building (next door to the FHC), and to approximately 200 terminals scattered around the church headquarters. But as of early 1998, there is still no remote access.

In the early 1980s, the church began to set up Family History Centers around the world. In 1988, they started selling the databases on microfiche. And in 1991, they released the databases on CD-ROM to local FHCs, followed by various societies and libraries. The New England Historic Genealogical Society has a copy of the databases at its Boston headquarters, as does the California State Sutro Library in San Francisco. More sites are certain to follow suit. In 1994, the church began testing the CD-ROMs for in-home use, but so far the CD-ROMs remain unavailable to individuals. Discussions are underway about online access, but it isn't here yet.

The pattern is clear: more access through more means. However, the LDS is very cautious about this. They are taking one very small step at a time, then evaluating the results before moving to the next step. The church has yet to work out the legal issues involved in making their databases widely available online. They are also very concerned with delivering a quality product that is useful to church members and the rest of the world. The main concern is to not turn out a bad product.

There are no plans to make the Ancestral File available to the general public.

To get the latest information on obtaining the IGI on CD-ROM, send mail to this address:

FamilySearch Support Unit
50 East North Temple
Salt Lake City, UT 84150

A Visit to a Family History Center

Terry Morgan, genealogy forum staff member at America Online (screen name GFA Terry), is also a volunteer at the two Family History Centers in Huntsville, Alabama. According to her, the setup at these FHCs is typical. Terry gave Libbi a guided tour of one of the FHCs.

"The best way to find one near you is to look in the White Pages of the phone book for the nearest LDS church," Morgan said. "Call them and find out where the nearest FHC is and the hours. Honestly, since the hours vary so much from place to place, the best time to call is Sunday morning around 10; everyone is at church then!" If you call any other time, give the staffers lots of rings to answer the phones—they may be on the other side of the church from the FHC. Or you could write to the main LDS library (at the address listed in the previous section), and ask for the latest list of FHCs. The larger centers are listed at the LDS Web site.

There's also an excellent list of FHCs on the Web at http://www. cyndislist.com/lds.htm (Fig. 9-2). This list is maintained by Cyndi Howells and is part of Cyndi's List of Genealogy Sites on the Internet.

Figure 9-2
Cyndi's List has an excellent collection of information on FHCs, including the locations of hundreds of them.

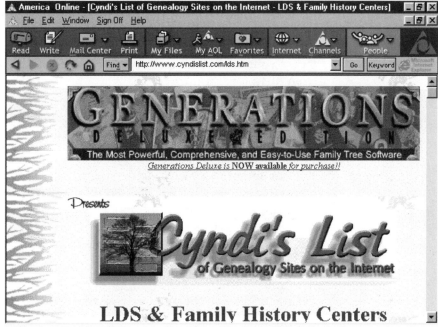

http://www.cyndislist.com/

All Family History Centers are branches of the main LDS Family History Library in Salt Lake City. A typical FHC is a couple of rooms at the local Mormon church with one to ten computers, a like number of microfilm and microfiche readers, and a collection of books (usually atlases), manuals, and how-to genealogy guides.

The FHC Libbi visited had two IBM-compatible computers that shared a printer in a room with a small library of about 25 reference books. In another room there were two film and two fiche readers. A cork bulletin board held the latest brochures of genealogical techniques from the Salt Lake City Family History Library. Visitors to the FHC are asked to sign in and out.

In some FHCs, Terry explained, the computers are networked so that patrons can easily share the CD-ROMs. In the future, perhaps before the turn of the century, FHCs could have direct satellite links to the main FHL, giving them access to the latest data while cutting distribution time. Keep your fingers crossed. Today, most centers have the IGI and the FamilySearch program set available for visitors to use.

"Some centers offer training on the programs, some insist they train you before you start using the computers, and some just help if you ask," Morgan said. "We offer help if you ask here." As of this writing, the programs won't run under Microsoft Windows, but Morgan said that might change in the future.

In the typical FHC setup, you must reserve a computer and a block of time to use it. You can usually print out the results of your research for a nickel a page. Some centers allow you to bring your own floppy disks to record your results, while others insist you buy certified virus-free disks from them for a nominal fee.

The Databases

The computers at an FHC are set up to run FamilySearch, a set of programs that can search five CD-ROM databases. When you begin, you'll see an opening screen with eight options.

- Tutorial
- Ancestral File
- International Genealogical Index
- United States Social Security Index
- Military Index

■ Family History Library Catalog

■ Scottish Church Records Index

■ TempleReady

■ Personal Ancestral File

The first items in the list are the ones visitors use most often. We've listed them in the order you're most likely to want to use them. However, before we examine the most useful items, we'll take a brief look at the last two entries.

TempleReady is a program that's only of interest to church members. It helps them to prepare genealogical records for Mormon religious rites.

Personal Ancestral File is a well-known LDS program for working with personal genealogical data. Its greatest strengths are GEDCOMs and family groups. You can buy a copy of Personal Ancestral File through various outlets. If you're considering it, you can go to a nearby FHC to test-drive the software before you spend your money. The FamilySearch tutorial has helpful information on how to run Personal Ancestral File. Now on to the most popular parts of FamilySearch.

Tutorial.   The tutorial takes you through the database programs step-by-step, showing you in detail how each one works. It'll take about 15 minutes to work through the tutorial, and it's time well spent. Once you finish here you're ready to explore the rest of the programs.

Ancestral File.   This is a good place to begin your research, because it has finished genealogies. It's similar to GEDCOM databases you find on the World Wide Web. This database has pedigree charts of family group sheets donated by people from all over the world, usually in GEDCOM format. "It's important to remember," said Terry Morgan, "this information is not verified. It's best to consider this an opinion file. The Salt Lake City FHL can't check out each of the millions of submissions, but they will try to find and merge duplicate pedigree lines and they accept corrections that you choose to submit." Anyone can donate data to the AF, even nonmembers, so you're likely to find some good clues on where to start looking for more data.

To search with Ancestral File, you enter a name (required) and an event date (not required). Once you run a search, you select a record from a menu of hits, records that match the search criteria you entered. The program then returns the name and address of the person who submitted the data. Note that the address is the person's address when they submitted the data, not necessarily their current address. Note also that an upcoming upgrade to the Ancestral File program will cause it to show more documentation for entries.

You can print the results of an AF search (press **F2**) or save them to diskette. You can also use Ancestral File to produce family group sheets.

If you find errors or omissions in the AF, you're invited to submit your data to the FHL in Salt Lake City. According to Morgan, the AF CD-ROMs should include your changes within a year or two after you submit them.

International Genealogical Index. The first thing to remember about the International Genealogical Index is that the data comes primarily from Mormon church members. The data isn't stored in pedigree form, but this database contains more names than the Ancestral File.

You search the IGI by submitting a name (required), date (optional), and location (optional). Once the program returns its results, you can print them or save them to floppy disk as you did for Ancestral File. The results will include call numbers for documentation of each entry.

Remember that the Mormon church is worldwide, and the data in the IGI comes from all over the planet. If the documentation for a particular record comes from France, it's likely that the documentation will be in French!

United States Social Security Index. The United States government made Social Security records public domain. The LDS put the information on CD-ROM and designed a program that lets you search the records. The result is a powerful tool for genealogists.

This database contains very good death records for 1962 through 1997, as well as some records back to 1937. You should realize that not all deaths are recorded here. Only those deaths that were reported to the Social Security Administration appear in this database.

Beyond death records, this database holds birth dates, last known place of residence, location the death payment was sent to, the state the recipient lived in when the Social Security number was issued, and the Social Security number itself. You search this database by name.

Military Index. The Military Index is another set of public-domain records created by the U.S. government and computerized by the Mormons. It contains information about U.S. citizens who died in the Vietnam and Korean wars.

In this database, you'll find birth and death dates, rank and serial number, as well as any other vital statistics the military had for each person.

This data may include marital status, state of residence, and similar information.

Family History Library Catalog. This option deals with a CD-ROM containing the entire contents of the main Family History Library. Each year the church updates this CD-ROM and the microfiche that contains the same data. You have several options when you start this program: Search Locality, Browse Locality, Surname Search, Film/Fiche Number, Computer Number Search, and Tutorial.

SEARCH LOCALITY. Enter a place, a country, state, county, city, or township and you'll get back a list of every record in the library that mentions that locality. The returned information will include the author's name, date, format of the record, and call number. You can also search on a subject by entering the subject (say Mayflower or Land Grant) into the locality field.

BROWSE LOCALITY. This option results in more hits than the same query would for Search Locality. "I recommend using the microfiche to 'browse' through a subject," said Morgan. "If you just want information from a particular state or country, you could pull out the 'Nebraska' fiche and read it all in perhaps an easier way than using the computer." This is the one case in which Terry felt that microfiche was the best way to find something.

SURNAME SEARCH. This surname search also allows you to add keywords to your search. Once you search on a surname, you can press **F6** to add keywords to narrow the search. In addition, you can search by author and title using the surname search.

FILM/FICHE NUMBER. If you know the call number of a microfilm or microfiche, this option will tell you what else is on that film or fiche. Sometimes widely divergent items are included on one roll; sometimes the roll is filled with closely related items.

COMPUTER NUMBER SEARCH. If you know the computer index number of a particular record, this option will display all the data in that record.

TUTORIAL. The tutorial is a guided tour of the catalog search system.

Scottish Church Records. The Presbyterian Church of Scotland is the source for this data. It consists of almost 10 million names from parish registers and similar records maintained by the Church of Scotland between the late 1500s and 1854.

Other Resources

Beyond the computerized data, FHCs offer some other valuable resources. "A very good resource is the Research Outlines," said Morgan. "Each Family History Center has a full set.... They're also for sale from the main library in Salt Lake City."

The outlines cover every U.S. state and Canadian province as well as dozens of other countries. They're guidelines and suggestions for how to do research in their areas. In each outline you'll find important addresses and tips and techniques that might be particularly appropriate for the area covered by the outline.

Another resource is the word lists. As mentioned before, you may find that the source information you need is in another language. The word lists contain translations of the words genealogists are most concerned with, in several dozen languages. You can buy your own word lists or borrow the reference set at the FHC.

The Mormon Connection

Right now, you have to go to your nearest FHC to take advantage of all the resources they have to offer. If your local FHC has a staff of knowledgeable volunteers like Terry Morgan, it's well worth your time to leave your PC and modem behind for a while and investigate these resources. Another reason to try out your local FHC is that someday, if time, money, and security issues get resolved, you might soon be able to dial up an FHC. If that ever happens, you'll be glad you're already up to speed on the resources available from the Church of Jesus Christ of Latter-Day Saints.

APPENDIX A

THE GENSERV SYSTEM

Would you like to search over 12 million names in more than 9000 GED-COM databases, all in one location and all accessible by Web or e-mail? If so, GenServ may be the system for you.

GenServ is an attempt to use distributed networking to share and disseminate genealogical information. But be warned—the information you find is only as reliable as the people submitting it. GenServ doesn't require that information come from a certified genealogist, nor does it include original sources or any form of proof. In fact, you should read carefully the disclaimer at http://www.genserv.com/gs/gsdic.htm, which states that the submitter owns the data and the submitter is responsible for it.

What Is It?

GenServ stands for Genealogical GEDCOM Server. Each GEDCOM database contains standard genealogical information about a family—names, birth dates and locations, marriages, and so forth. GenServ lets you search all of its thousands of GEDCOMs simultaneously using simple commands. Figure A-1 shows the World Wide Web home page of the GenServ system at http://www.genserv.com.

Understand, however, that there is no way to eliminate or merge individuals found in more than one GEDCOM database. In fact, many duplicated individual records are known to exist. The value is in seeing how they are related to different people.

How Does It Work?

The information in GenServ comes from anyone who wishes to participate, but none of it is checked, verified, or validated. The only authentication you'll find here is whatever submitters included in notes attached to the records in the GEDCOMs.

Once you have subscribed to GenServ, it's easy to do research. You can send information requests to the system through the Web site, or by e-mail.

Figure A-1
The GenServ Web site
is one of the ways you
can explore the sys-
tem's large collection
of GEDCOM data-
bases.

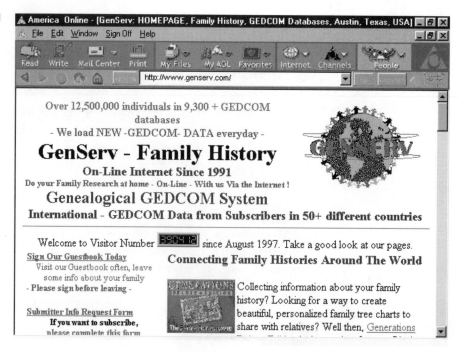

Figure A-1
The GenServ Web site is one of the ways you can explore the system's large collection of GEDCOM databases.

GenServ allows you to search for names alone, or you can add qualifiers like born after or died before. You can also tell the system to include specific data fields out of the 14 fields that are stored for each entry.

For a complete list of commands, go to http://www.genserv.com/gs/genhow2.htm and read the file GENHOW2 before you submit your information request. To be sure you have the latest version of GEN-HOW2, send a blank e-mail message to genhow2@genserv.com.

Should I Subscribe?

The big advantage of GenServ is clear: easy searching of over 9000 GED-COM databases. Unfortunately, there are some disadvantages to subscribing to GenServ.

First, it costs money. With all the free and low-cost resources on AOL and the Net, you may not want to spend the money to subscribe.

Second, as we've already stated, the information in GenServ is not verified in any way. Whatever GEDCOM information someone sends to the system gets added to the databases on the assumption that the person submitting the GEDCOM has verified it.

Third, you must submit a GEDCOM to GenServ before you can subscribe to the system. While this may not be a problem for serious hobbyists or professionals, it does require you to use a genealogical software program that can generate GEDCOMs GenServ can understand.

NOTE   *The What is GenServ? page at the GenServ Web site contains a commitment not to redistribute the GEDCOM databases you provide to the system as a condition of membership. The only use that is made of your GEDCOM databases is to search them for genealogical information.*

There are a few things you can do to see if GenServ is likely to have the specific information you are looking for. First, you can do a sample search. The GenServ system allows you to do a one-time surname search by going to http://www.Genserv.com/gs3/samplesearch.html and entering a surname and e-mail address. The system then searches for that surname and within an hour or so e-mails you a report on that surname. Figure A-2 shows a tiny part of the results of a surname search on MANN.

You can also ask the system to do any number of surname counts. In a surname count, GenServ reports to you the number of entries it has for that surname. Just enter the surname in question and your e-mail address at http://www.genserv.com/gs3/samplecount.html. Within a short while GenServ will e-mail you with the number of entries it has for that surname.

The next step in testing the GenServ system calls for more work on your part. You can go through the subscription process, including creating a GEDCOM and sending it to GenServ, then sign up for a free two-month trial subscription. This gives you the ability to submit up to 12 requests an hour during the trial period. You do not get to see the submitter information for the records you get back, but you do get to give the system a good trial run and determine if there's a lot of good stuff for you.

Given the pros and cons listed here, it's up to you to decide whether a subscription to GenServ is worthwhile.

Figure A-2
GenServ allows any-
one to do a single sur-
name search without
becoming a
subscriber.

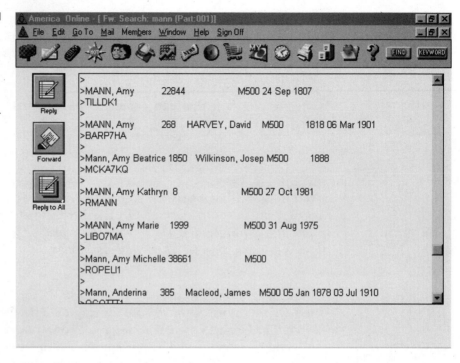

How Do I Subscribe?

Cliff Manis, the originator of this project, strongly urges potential subscribers to first fill out the form at http://www.genserv.com/gs3/inforeq
.html. This way your contact information will be exactly as you wish, and
people can contact you about your data more easily.

There are four steps you must take to subscribe to GenServ. You must
complete all four steps before becoming a subscriber. The four steps are
described in detail at http://www.genserv.com/gs/gsh2sub.htm; here I've
included a short summary of the process. Figure A-3 shows the beginning
of this page.

Step 1: Create a GEDCOM Database

Unless you happen to have one lying around somewhere, you need to generate a GEDCOM database. This may take a while, but you cannot join

Figure A-3

Subscribing to
GenServ is a four-step
process. You can get
complete details on
this page and the
pages linked to this
page.

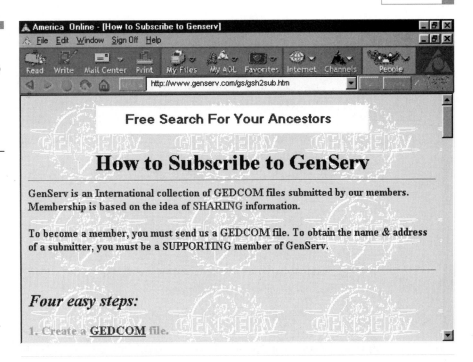

GenServ without first submitting a GEDCOM database. The instructions
on the Subscription Web page tell you how to export a GEDCOM database from any of the common genealogical programs.

Step 2: Send the GEDCOM Database to GenServ

Once you have a GEDCOM to submit, you should go to the How to Send
Us Your GEDCOM Data page at http://www.genserv.com/gs/gensdata.htm.
You can submit a GEDCOM database by e-mail, FTP, or postal mail. A new
feature is the ability to upload the GEDCOM file via the form at
http://www.genserv.com/gs3/upload.html. You must read the upload HELP
file before using this.

   Whatever format you use, be sure to follow the submission instructions exactly. You can read the instructions online or have the system
e-mail them to you. Just click on the appropriate link to get the information you need.

Step 3: Fill in and Submit the GenServ Information Request Form

The GenServ Information Request Form tells the people who run GenServ a lot about your computerized genealogical activities. Only the GenServ staff uses this information—it is not given away or sold to other companies. You can get to this form by following the appropriate link from the How to Subscribe to GenServ page, or you can go there directly by entering http://www.genserv.com/gs3/inforeq.html.

Step 4: Choose Your Membership Plan

There are four subscription plans to choose from. At a minimum, each plan requires that you submit at least one GEDCOM. Additional details of each plan are listed here.

Trial Subscription.   You will receive a two-month free trial. You can submit up to 12 information requests an hour, but the system won't tell you anything about the persons who submitted the information in the hits you get back. You also do not get access to the GenServ subscriber Web pages. Only one trial subscription is allowed per person/e-mail address, regardless of the number of GEDCOM databases that person submits to GenServ.

Regular Subscription.   For $12.00 (US), you get a one-year subscription with up to 12 requests per hour. You get to see the submitter information associated with any hits, and you have access to the subscriber Web pages.

Senior Subscription.   This is the same as a regular subscription, except the price is $6.00 (US) per year. Up to 12 requests per hour. You get to see the submitter information associated with any hits, and you have access to the subscriber Web pages.

Prime Sponsor Subscription.   For $35.00 (US) (or higher as donations are welcomed), you get a one-year subscription with up to 60 requests per hour. You get to see the submitter information associated with any hits, and you have access to the subscriber Web pages.

Once you send in your GEDCOM, and the staff at GenServ successfully uploads it to the system, you will receive membership information. This includes a GenServ ID and instructions on how to access the system as a subscriber.

How you submitted your GEDCOM database determines how long it takes to get your membership processed.

FTP—within 24 hours

E-mail—within 3 days

Postal Mail—within 3 weeks

Send your subscription check to:

Cliff Manis
P.O. Box 33937
San Antonio TX 78265-3937

Preparing Your GEDCOM

While your genealogical software can prepare a GEDCOM database for you, don't run off willy-nilly! There are things you should do to ensure that your GEDCOM database can be read by the GenServ system and that the data you provide is of real value to others.

Have your software create a database made up of data you have accumulated and analyzed in your researches, including not only basic data such as names and dates, but also any Notes fields. Be sure the database is the result of your own researches, not simply one produced by automatic extraction from some other system such as the IGI CD-ROM system. The data you supply remains your property, and will not be provided to anyone else as a GEDCOM, so you needn't worry about losing control of your original work.

When GenServ searches, it does so on the entire set of databases that have been submitted to it. But each database remains separate and associated with the name of its author. So, if you find new or better data in the future, you can withdraw a GEDCOM database you previously submitted and replace it with a new one. This is a plus for the system, but doing things this way has certain implications. In particular, it means there is no way to eliminate or merge individuals found in more than one GEDCOM database. In fact, many duplicates are known to exist in the GenServ system.

In theory, a GEDCOM database exported from any genealogical database management system should be acceptable to any system that claims to be able to import GEDCOM files. In practice, so many differences exist between the GEDCOM formats used by various systems that a GEDCOM database produced by one system may not load correctly, or at all, on some other system.

So once you create your GEDCOM, you should test it before sending it off to GenServ. The test will show whether your genealogical database management system (your genealogy program) has created a GEDCOM database GenServ is likely to be able to understand.

The test involves trying to import your GEDCOM into one of the following programs:

- PAF (LDS), version 2.1 or later
- GIM (Genealogical Information Manager), version 2.0 or later
- Brother's Keeper, any version from 1992 or later
- LifeLines, the UNIX Genealogical Program, any version

You should be able to download one or more of these programs by FTP from the programs directory in the genealogy area at ftp.cac.psu.edu (128.118.2.23). Some of the files available by FTP are visible in Fig. A-4.

If you use Family Tree Maker, be sure to save your GEDCOM database as a PAF file (version 4 or 5, using IBM PC character set) with no indent

Figure A-4

Test your GEDCOM database with programs from this genealogy programs directory.

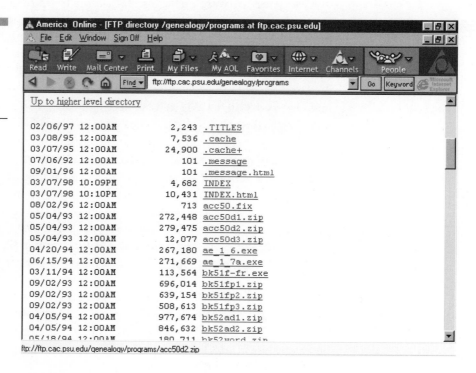

and with abbreviated tags before checking to see that the database can be imported correctly.

If you use ROOTS IV, be sure to save your GEDCOM database as a ROOTS 3 GEDCOM file, as GenServ cannot read ROOTS IV GEDCOM files.

Special Tips on Submitting Your GEDCOM

- If you send your GEDCOM database to GenServ by postal mail, you must include a piece of paper on which you have typed your e-mail address, postal street address, city, state, ZIP code, country, and telephone number.

- Apple Macintosh users should use Apple File Exchange or an equivalent program to produce MS-DOS—compatible floppy disks when sending GEDCOM databases by postal mail.

- If you have a GEDCOM database with over 30,000 surnames, you should contact Cliff Manis for special instructions on sending your GEDCOM to GenServ. The system has databases containing more than 50,000 surnames, but such large files require special handling. You can e-mail Cliff at admin@genserv.com.

- GenServ is very interested in complete GEDCOM databases, so include all your notes and other tags.

- The data and documents on the system are the responsibility of the individual authors of the GEDCOM databases, not GenServ. Keep this in mind when you're trying to decide how much weight to give to the information you find here.

- The data on the system belongs to the authors of the GEDCOM databases it comes from.

- It is the responsibility of individual contributors to obey all applicable laws and standards governing the contents of their GEDCOM files.

- The GenServ staff will not try to find your e-mail address if you do not send it to them. If they don't know your e-mail address, they cannot provide any help to you.

- Updates to the GEDCOM databases on the system are welcome at six-month intervals. Do not update your files more frequently than that.

- Be sure to read the GenServ documentation carefully before attempting to use the system. You can get the documentation from their Web site, or by FTP from ftp.cac.psu.edu. You can also get the system to e-mail you the documentation by sending an e-mail message to gen-info@genserv.com.

- If you send your GEDCOM database by postal mail, e-mail Cliff Manis that same day and let him know it is coming. Cliff can use the address in this e-mail message to contact you, either to let you know that your GEDCOM database was loaded successfully or to tell you that there was a problem.

- To update the data in one of your GEDCOM databases, follow the same procedure as for submitting new information, but label the e-mail message or floppy disk UPDATE TO <<the name of the GEDCOM database you want to update>>.

APPENDIX B

One of the reasons to get involved in online genealogy is to share the information you have and find information you don't have. To make that easier, there are several standard formats for transmitting genealogical information. This appendix addresses tiny tafels.

What Is a Tiny Tafel?

A tiny tafel is a format for telling the world what genealogical data you have. It isn't a format for exchanging the data; instead, it alerts others to the existence of the data and tells them how to contact you. A tiny tafel exists to indicate interest, to let people know what you have and what you want in a quick, standardized way. Though computer programs can read tiny tafels to make these connections, you, too, can read and understand what tiny tafels have to say. All you need to do is learn the format, which you'll do shortly.

Paul Anderek proposed the tiny tafel (TT) format in an article, "Tiny-Tafel for Database Scope Indexing," in the April-May-June 1986 issue of *Genealogical Computing* as an alternative to the numerical Ahnentafel format. The advantage of tiny tafels over ahnentafels would be size; the tiny tafel would be a shorthand representation of the data. Instead of listing every known ancestor in a particular surname line, the TT would instead show a range for the surname, in dates, locations, and Soundex codes. An entire surname line would be summarized in a single tiny tafel line. The top of the file would have contact information for exchanging the actual data. Furthermore, the data fields in a TT would be fixed in size and type, making it easy for various computer programs to read the files. This would make matching tiny tafels much easier.

The tiny tafel standard format was first used in Commsoft's Roots program, but now several genealogical data programs have built-in or add-on utilities to output a tiny tafel from your data. As the format of tiny tafels is rather unforgiving of typos, you should probably have a program generate your TT rather than trying to do one by hand. However, you do need to know how to read a tiny tafel and what each column and line mean.

What Is the Tiny Tafel Matching System?

Warning: As of this writing the Tiny Tafel Matching System (TTMS) cannot be reached through America Online or any Internet connection. Your modem must dial directly into a participating bulletin board system (BBS) to get access to the TTMS. Some of the terms in this section may be unfamiliar to you as they apply to a different corner of the online world than the rest of the book. The information in this section is provided for your own exploration and to prepare you in case the TTMS does someday become available through AOL or the Net.

The Tiny Tafel Matching System is a system whereby tiny tafels from around the world can be searched for free. The system works through participating bulletin board systems. You can find a participating BBS by searching the National Genealogy Society's list of genealogical BBSs, then logging onto nearby boards until you find one that is involved. Look for boards that include DA as one of their echoes. You could also ask around at local computer user groups and genealogy clubs to find the closest participating BBS.

Anatomy of a Tiny Tafel

Tiny tafels are easier to use if you know how to read the data stored in them. The tiny tafel file is a plain text file, so you can open it with any word processor. The contents of a TT file are divided into two sections: originator information and data records.

Originator Information

The first few lines are information about the tiny tafel's originator. Each line in this section contains specific information, with the first character on the line specifying what the information on the line is. The following list describes the possible information lines:

N is the first character of the line that holds the name of the originator.

A appears first on an address line. There can be as many *A* lines as necessary to hold the postal mail address of the originator.

T is the telephone number of the originator.

B is the name of the BBS the originator uses.

C is for the communications setup of the BBS.

S lines list e-mail addresses on commercial online services. There can be up to five *S* lines.

D is the size of floppy disk the originator can use to exchange data.

F is the format line, which describes the software that formatted this tiny tafel.

R These are remark lines. There can be as many *R* lines as necessary.

Z This line contains the total number of records (lines) in this TT.

Only the *N* and *Z* lines are required. The others are all optional. If the actual number of records in the TT doesn't match the number on the *Z* line, the TTMS software assumes the tiny tafel file is corrupt. This is one of the reasons why it is best to let software generate your tiny tafels for you.

The first part of a typical tiny tafel file might look like this:

N   Elizabeth P. Crowe

A   619 Mountain Gap Road

A   Huntsville, AL 35803

T   205-555-5555

S   etravel@delphi.com

S   LibbiC@aol.com

S   lcrowe@iquest.com

C   28.8K/O/Zmodem

D   3/1.4M/DSDD

F   BK for Windows

R   I can also exchange data via fax

Z   ....

The *Z* line would contain the final count of the data lines in the TT file.

Data Records

The majority of most tiny tafel files consists of data records. This is the good stuff. In this part of the file, each line represents a separate record, and each column of each line is significant. The records are divided into fields, most of which are of fixed length and occupy certain columns.

The data are divided this way:

Column	Description
1–4	Soundex code for the name with the highest interest level
5	A blank space
6–9	Birth year of earliest ancestor
10	Interest flag for this ancestral line (The interest flags are one character each: a space ( ) signifies no interest; a period (.) means low interest; a colon (:) means moderate interest; an asterisk (*) means highest interest level.)
11–14	Latest descendant's birth year
15	Interest flag for the descendant end of the family line (Uses the same flags as column 10)
16–16+	The surname string area, which has variable length (Up to five surnames can be added per line, starting at column 16. But remember to save some room on the line for place names.)
16+–end	Place names for the birth of the earliest ancestor and latest descendant (A backslash (\) means a place related to the ancestor, while a forward slash (/) indicates a place related to the descendant.)

So, a typical TT line could be:

K530 1770*1996 Kennedy\IR/Boston MA/St. Louis MO/San Francisco CA

Translated into English, this line says the following. The Soundex code is K530. The submitter is very interested in this family line in the 1700s but not interested at all in the present generation. The Kennedy this record refers to came from Ireland to Boston, Massachusetts. The family moved from St. Louis to San Francisco. Once you get used to it, the tiny tafel format is very easy to read.

Tips and Rules

Here are some tips and rules to follow when creating a tiny tafel file.

■ You must enter dates, and they must be valid dates. The matching system requires dates to function.

- If listing the first and last of a line hides some migration, you can break the surname into two records. Remember this is a shorthand version of your research—you should render the data the best you can but not worry about cramming every conceivable item into the records.

- If you don't know an exact location, put something there like the state or continent. The more information you give, the better the chance you have of finding someone with similar interests.

- If you are generating a tiny tafel file by hand, or are editing a computer-generated one, make sure you get the *Z* line right.

Submitting Tiny Tafels

The point of tiny tafels is to alert the world to the fact that you have, or are interested in, certain genealogical information. So it makes sense to put your tiny tafel files where others can find them. There are three good places to submit your TT files: the Genealogy Forum on AOL, certain genealogical newsgroups, and the tiny tafel matching system (TTMS).

On AOL

On AOL, you can submit your TT file to the Ancestors file library. In the Genealogy Forum main menu, double click **File Libraries Center**. Now click the **Ancestors** button to see the list of file libraries in the Ancestor category. Now find Tafel Library 1 and upload your tiny tafel. Once you upload a TT file to this library, it should appear there in a few days.

You should also look in the Surname Center (double click **Surname Center** on the Genealogy Forum main menu) under the specific surname you are working on. Some surnames, like Smith, have their own tiny tafel library.

To the TTMS

You can also submit your tiny tafel files to the TTMS. As mentioned earlier, the TTMS is free. BBSs that provide access to the TTMS are required to do so for no charge, although many sysops require you to post a TT of your own before you are allowed to use the TTMS.

Submitting tiny tafels is one of the three functions of the TMS software that does the work for the TTMS. The other two functions are *instant searches*, which use only surnames and only search the BBS you are connected to, and *offline searches*, which allow more complicated queries and search all the bulletin board systems participating in TTMS.

You start a search by selecting the type of search you wish to run. You then answer a few questions, and the system begins its search. Figure B-1 shows the results of an instant search.

As Fig. B-1 shows, the result of an instant search is a list of hits, the lines in any tiny tafels on this BBS that match your search criteria. To see the details of a particular hit, you enter the line number, and the system responds by giving you the data for that line. Figure B-2 shows what happens when you enter the line number of a hit.

Instant searches provide instant (well, within a few minutes anyway) gratification, but they are a less efficient way to search. Because you do instant searches online, you tie up the BBS while the search is in progress and may rack up extra phone charges while you wait for the results to come back.

Offline searches take longer but are worth the wait. When you submit a query for an offline search, it goes out to every BBS in the TTMS before

Figure B-1

An instant search can give you results in minutes but only for the BBS you are connected to.

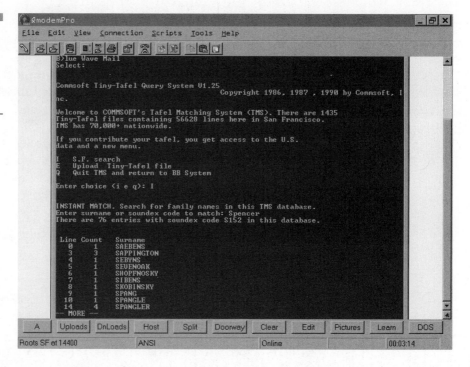

Figure B-2
If the TTMS finds a
record you are inter-
ested in, you can get
the system to display
the entire tiny tafel.

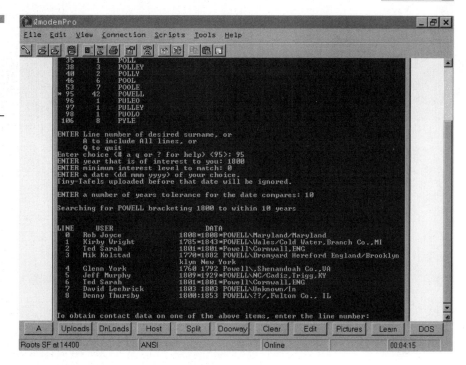

Figure B-2
If the TTMS finds a record you are interested in, you can get the system to display the entire tiny tafel.

a report is generated. This takes a few days, but the reports you get back cover the entire system, greatly increasing your chances of finding relevant information.

To retrieve your reports, log back onto the BBS you conducted the search from, then get back into the TTMS. The system will then tell you whether there are any reports waiting for you. You can view the reports online or download them to your computer to read offline. We strongly recommend the latter as these reports can reach 100 pages in length. Your hits are listed by BBS.

Glossary

address The information that identifies a particular computer or a particular Web page. *See* **URL**.

Address bar The area of a browser window where you enter the address of the Web page you want to open next.

AF *See* **Ancestral File**.

Ahnentafel A pedigree table for a person's ancestors. It includes the full name, as well as the date and location of birth, marriage, and death for all known ancestors. Uses a specific numbering scheme to identify each individual in the family tree. The term means *ancestor table* in German.

American Standard Code for Information Interchange (ASCII) A simple means of storing numbers and letters in a computer.

analog Analog signals are signals that vary continuously in level. Sound is a perfect example of an analog signal.

Ancestral File™ (AF) A compilation of genealogies containing millions of names and family pedigrees, primarily for deceased people. The Ancestral File is the property of the Mormons, but can be searched at their Family History Centers™.

anonymous FTP A means to make files on a computer available to people who don't have an account on that computer. An anonymous FTP site normally will not allow you to change the files available at the site or contribute files to it—you can only copy files from it. *See also* **File Transfer Protocol**.

Archie A program you can use to search for files in FTP databases.

archive A collection of files or data. An archive in AOL or on the Web is usually a directory containing related files.

ASCII *See* **American Standard Code for Information Interchange**.

Asynchronous Transfer Mode (ATM) A high-speed data transfer standard that may someday find its way into home use.

ATM *See* **Asynchronous Transfer Mode**.

backbone The interconnections that form the main information channel on a network. In most cases, the backbone is high speed, can carry large amounts of information, and is continuously active.

bandwidth   The amount of data that can flow through a network. The higher the bandwidth, the more data can flow at any time. For networks with lots of simultaneous users—like AOL and the Internet—the higher the bandwidth, the faster the network is for each user.

baud   A measure of data transmission speed. It is not equivalent to bits per second, but to state changes per second.

BBS   *See* **Bulletin Board System**.

bit   The smallest unit of information in a computer. A bit can have two values, 0 or 1. All information in your computer, on AOL, or on the Internet is composed of bits.

Bitnet   Originally a cooperative computer network interconnecting over 2300 academic and research institutions in 32 countries. Bitnet has become a part of the Internet, although some schools still restrict user access to the original Bitnet computers.

browse   To move around the World Wide Web with the help of a Web browser.

browser   A client program that lets you view files on the World Wide Web. Browsers such as Internet Explorer also allow you to view FTP sites and other Internet services. Also called a Web browser or WWW browser.

Bulletin Board System (BBS)   An electronic bulletin board where people can read and post messages as well as upload and download files. Many BBSs can only be reached by a dial-up modem connection, while some are connected to the Internet.

cable modem   A type of modem that allows high-speed Internet (and AOL) access using a cable television system to carry the information.

CERN   The Swiss research group where Tim Berners-Lee came up with the basic design for the World Wide Web.

chat   A way to communicate with another computer user by typing messages in real time.

client   A computer or program that serves as the connection between a user and services or forums on an online service or the Internet.

client/server   A system where one computer acts as the client by requesting services from another computer, the server. Most of the time, the Internet and AOL function as client/server systems.

compression   Methods of reducing the size of a file. Smaller files take up less storage space and can be transferred more quickly by modem.

Some compressed files are actually collections of several files, all stored together as an archive. Most modems can compress files before transmitting them and decompress them after they receive them.

conference   A live online chat or echo session.

connect charge   The fee charged by AOL or an Internet Service Provider. Depending on your agreement with the service provider, this may be an hourly fee or a flat monthly charge.

Computer Research and Education Network (CREN)   The new name for the merged computer networks Bitnet and Computer Science Network (CSNET). The new network supports electronic mail and file transfers.

CREN   *See* **Computer Research and Education Network**.

cyberspace   The "place" you are when you are connected to America Online or the Internet.

database   An organized collection of information stored on a computer.

digital   A digital signal is one that consists of a stream (usually a *very long stream*) of ones and zeros. Computers and compact discs work with digital signals.

directory   A storage area that can hold files and other directories.

domain name server (DNS)   A computer that can translate a domain name into an IP address.

domain name   The name of a computer on the Internet. A domain name is the human-readable version of a computer's IP address. In a standard e-mail address, the part after the @ is the domain. If jdoe@aol.com is an e-mail address, aol.com is the domain.

door   A program that allows you to perform specific functions on a BBS. While a door is active, the BBS software does not run.

download   To copy e-mail messages, files, or other information from a remote computer to your computer.

echo   Messages related to a particular subject that are passed between BBSs that request them.

electronic mailing list   An online discussion group composed of e-mail messages. A list may have a moderator (a person who reviews each message before it appears in the list). To participate, you send commands to a listserv or listserver.

e-mail   *See* **electronic mail**.

electronic mail   Any of a number of systems that allow you to compose a message on one computer and transmit it across a network to another computer. Both AOL and the Internet support e-mail systems and can exchange e-mail with each other.

emoticons   Also known as smileys. Textual pictures used to convey emotions in e-mail messages. One example is the classic smiley face :-). See the next section for a collection of common emoticons.

FHC   *See* **Family History Center**.

Family History Center™   A Mormon facility that allows visitors to conduct genealogical research using the church's computerized genealogy databases.

File Transfer Protocol (FTP)   A system that allows you to upload and download files across the Internet.

file   A collection of information treated as a single unit by a computer. E-mail messages, Ahnentafel, and tiny tafels are examples of files you will encounter while doing genealogical research.

flame   An angry, nasty, or insulting message. When you send such a message to someone, you are *flaming* them. Flaming people will get you into trouble on AOL and other online services.

folder   *See* **directory**.

forum   An area on an online service where you can find information about a particular topic and sometimes chat with others who share your interest in the topic. The Genealogy Forum on AOL is an outstanding example of what a forum should be.

front-end software   A program that provides you with an interface to an online service like America Online.

FTP   *See* **File Transfer Protocol**.

gateway   A computer that routes messages and other data between two networks.

GEDCOM   The standard format for computerized genealogical information. It combines tagged data and pointers to related data. Stands for Genealogical Data Communications.

GIF   A format for graphics files. This is one of the formats that all Web browsers understand.

Gopher   A service that allows you to search for information on the Internet and presents that information to you in the form of menus.

History folder An area on your computer where the AOL Web browser stores information about the places you recently browsed on the Internet. This folder can grow quite large (megabytes).

home page The first page you see when you enter a Web site.

host computer In the context of networks, this is a computer that directly provides services to a user. This is in contrast to a network server, which provides services to a user through a host computer. When you are connected to AOL, the computer on your desk is the host computer, and the computers at AOL are network servers.

hot key In a BBS, a hot key is a command that takes a single keystroke to execute; you don't need to press Enter or Return to activate the command.

HTML *See* **Hypertext Markup Language**.

HTTP *See* **Hypertext Transfer Protocol**.

hub A BBS that transfers e-mail between one region and another.

hypertext A way to interconnect information. A hypertext isn't a sequential document like this book. Instead, information in a hypertext is linked to other relevant information, creating a web of information, possibly scattered across any number of computers located anywhere on Earth. Hence the term World Wide Web.

Hypertext Markup Language (HTML) The language used to write documents that appear on the World Wide Web. A Web browser reads HTML and translates it into the documents you see on the Web.

Hypertext Transfer Protocol (HTTP) The protocol or set of rules that determines how information should be transferred on the World Wide Web.

IGI *See* **International Genealogical Index**.

Integrated Services Digital Network (ISDN) A type of digital telephone and data system. Depending on how it is configured, an ISDN line can handle just computer data or simultaneous computer data and voice. The big advantage of using ISDN to connect to an online service or your ISP is speed. ISDN speeds can reach or exceed 128 Kbps.

International Genealogical Index® (IGI) A collection of birth, christening, and marriage information for millions of people who lived between the early 1500s and the early 1900s. The International Genealogical Index is the property of the Mormons, but can be searched at their Family History Centers.

International Telecommunications Union (ITU) The United Nations agency charged with establishing and coordinating world telecommunication standards.

Internet Protocol (IP) The rules that govern how computers communicate on the Internet. Messages are broken down into packets, which travel from the originating computer to the destination computer by the fastest path available at that instant. Once all the packets arrive at the destination, they are reassembled into a copy of the original message.

Internet Service Provider (ISP) An organization that provides users with a connection to the Internet. This organization takes care of all the complexity of maintaining a direct link to the Net. AOL is an ISP.

internet A network of computer networks.

Internet The Internet, with a capital I, is a worldwide network of networks. It is the largest network of computers in the world, connecting millions of machines. TCP/IP is the communications protocol computers use to communicate across the Internet.

INTERNIC The company that has contracted to administer certain functions of the Internet, such as maintaining domain names and assigning IP addresses.

intranet A private network that uses the TCP/IP protocol and appears to users as if it were a miniature version of the Internet. Access to intranets is normally restricted to members of a particular company or organization.

IP Address A set of numbers that identifies a particular computer connected to the Internet.

IP *See* **Internet Protocol**.

ISDN *See* **Integrated Services Digital Network**.

ISP *See* **Internet Service Provider**.

ITU *See* **International Telecommunications Union**.

Java A programming language developed by Sun Microsystems. Web developers can use Java to add capabilities to their pages that plain HTML can't match.

JPG A format for graphics files. This is one of the formats that is understood by virtually all Web browsers.

Jughead An Internet service used by Gopher to build menus of information.

Kbps Thousands of bits per second. Conventional modems may transfer data at 56 Kbps, while higher-speed systems like cable modems may transfer data at rates of thousands of Kbps.

LAN *See* **local area network**.

link A pointer to another file somewhere on the Internet.

list *See* **electronic mailing list**.

listserv *See* **listserver**.

listserver A program that manages an electronic mailing list.

local area network (LAN) A group of computers tied together by a high-speed connection. Many businesses now connect their computers to a LAN.

lurk To read the messages in a mailing list or echo without posting your own messages. Lurking is a good way to get a feel for a list or echo and is often encouraged for newcomers.

mail list *See* **electronic mailing list**.

MB *See* **Megabyte**.

Mbps Millions of bits per second. Cable modems can transfer data from the Internet or AOL at speeds in this range.

Megabyte (MB) A unit of measure for computer memory. Roughly equal to 1,000,000 characters.

menu bar The row of text at the very top of the America Online screen. Click on one of the words in the menu bar to see another menu of related options.

message thread *See* **thread**.

MNP One of the data compression standards for modems.

modem A device that converts between sound signals that the phone line can handle and electrical signals that a computer can handle. Modems are the most common way people connect to AOL or the Internet. Modem is short for modulator-demodulator.

moderator The person who is responsible for the content of a mailing list, echo, or forum. A moderator can control who is allowed to join, remove messages that are off topic or inappropriate, and discipline or eject members who don't follow the rules. Most of the mailing lists on the Internet do not have a moderator.

National Research and Education Network (NREN) This is a proposed research and education network that would be built on the existing Internet backbone.

Net   A common nickname for the Internet.

Network Information Center (NIC)   A facility that provides information and other forms of support to a particular network.

Network Interface Card (NIC)   A circuit card that sits inside your computer and allows it to communicate with high-speed devices like cable modems or a local area network.

network   Two or more interconnected computers. Many offices use local area networks, which connect a limited number of computers in a limited area. The Internet is a wide area network, connecting other networks around the world.

network server   A computer that provides services to a user across the network and through the user's host computer. The computers at AOL are network servers that communicate with the host computer on your desk through the phone network or the Internet.

newsgroup   Another means of sharing messages on the Internet. Similar to a mailing list except that messages are sent and received using special newsreader programs, not e-mail programs. AOL provides a newsreader program you can use to join any of the dozens of newsgroups dealing with genealogy. There are tens of thousands of newsgroups active on the Net, dealing with virtually any topic you can imagine.

newsreader   A program that allows you to read and post messages to and from a newsgroup. AOL has a built-in newsreader program.

NIC   *See* **Network Interface Card** or **Network Information Center**.

offline   The state of being disconnected from AOL, the Internet, or any other computer network.

Online Public Access Catalog (OPAC)   A term used to describe online card catalogs for libraries.

online   The state of being connected to AOL, the Internet, or any other computer network.

OPAC   *See* **Online Public Access Catalog**.

Open Systems Interconnection (OSI)   A developing standard for connecting computer systems. Computer networks that comply with the OSI standard can exchange information easily. As more genealogical information becomes available online, support for OSI will become more important.

OSI   *See* **Open Systems Interconnection**.

page   A single file or document as presented to you by a Web browser.

Plain Old Telephone Service (POTS)   This somewhat negative phrase is used to describe the standard voice telephone lines that run into your house.

Point of Presence (POP)   A location where phone calls from modems get converted into digital signals and entered into the AOL computer network. Messages from AOL to your computer are converted into analog signals and sent back across the phone line.

Point-to-Point Protocol (PPP)   This protocol makes dial-up IP connections possible.

POP   *See* **Point of Presence**.

POTS   *See* **Plain Old Telephone Service**.

PPP   *See* **Point-to-Point Protocol**.

protocol   A set of rules that tell computers how to communicate with each other. The protocol specifies the format of the information and the procedures by which it is transferred.

remote access   The ability to connect to a distant computer. Telnet is a form of remote access.

Serial Line IP (SLIP)   A system that allows computers to use the Internet Protocol (IP) with a standard telephone line and a high-speed modem.

search engine   A Web site that allows you to conduct searches of the Internet. Search engines can contain constantly updated information about millions of Web and FTP sites, as well as newsgroups, mailing lists, and other resources. AOL NetFind is a search engine that American Online makes available to the Internet community free of charge.

shareware   Try-before-you-buy software. The authors of these programs distribute them to the world at little or no cost. They then require people to pay for the software if those people decide to continue using the software after a specified evaluation period. Some genealogy software is distributed as shareware.

signature   A short text message you can create that is then automatically attached to the end of every message you send. Long signatures tend to be irritating and waste the resources of AOL or the Internet transmitting useless material. *See also* **tagline**.

SLIP   *See* **Serial Line IP**.

smileys Also known as emoticons. Textual pictures used to convey emotions in e-mail messages. One example is the classic smiley face :-). See the next section for a collection of common smileys.

spam An inappropriate e-mail message or newsgroup post that is sent to large numbers of newsgroups. While this term is widely used, it is considered inappropriate by the people who produce the food product of the same name.

spider A program that examines Web sites and returns relevant information about them to a search engine. Spiders help keep the information in a search engine current, and are the only way to keep up with the incredible amount of new and changed information on the Internet.

Status bar The bar at the bottom of a Web browser window. It's an area where the browser displays messages telling you what it is doing now.

sysop A system operator for a forum, BBS, or echo. Sysops ensure that everything keeps working, and may also serve as a moderator, and contributor.

tagline A short, pithy statement tagged onto the end of an e-mail message. Example: *It's only a hobby, only a hobby, only a.... See also* **signature**.

T-1 A digital circuit that can transfer computer data at 1.544 Mbps.

T-3 A digital circuit that can transfer 28 times as much data as a T-1 line.

TCP/IP *See* **Transmission Control Protocol/Internet Protocol**.

telnet A service that gives you remote access to a distant computer. When you are connected with telnet, it is as if you are using a terminal attached directly to the remote computer instead of far away on the Internet.

thread A sequence of messages related to a specific subject; analogous to a conversation. Also called a message thread.

tiny tafel (TT) A standard format for describing the contents of a family history database. The data can be read by machine or by a human. Except for the names and optional information, all the data in the TT is of a fixed length to allow for easier computer manipulation.

title bar The bar at the top of a window. It contains the title of the page or document that is visible in the window.

toolbar A row of icons that runs across the top of the AOL screen. Each icon is a shortcut to an important area or feature of America Online.

Transmission Control Protocol/Internet Protocol (TCP/IP) The combined set of protocols that computers must use to communicate directly with other computers connected to the Internet.

TT *See* **tiny tafel**.

upload To transfer messages or files from your computer to another computer. Certain locations on AOL and the Internet allow you to upload genealogical information.

Uniform Resource Locator (URL) A standard addressing scheme for finding things on the World Wide Web and the Internet.

URL *See* **Uniform Resource Locator**.

Usenet A network connected to the Internet. Primarily of interest as the storage area of most of the newsgroups you can reach using the Internet.

V.32 A data compression standard for modems.

Veronica An indexing system designed to make using Gopher easier. It allows you to search Gopher sites anywhere in the world.

video clip A bit of audio and video digitized for use on a computer.

Web browser *See* **browser**.

Web Server A computer that stores Web pages and delivers a copy of them to any program requesting it.

Web *See* **World Wide Web**.

World Wide Web (WWW or Web) This is the HTML portion of the Internet. It consists of documents and hyperlinks that connect them. Web documents may contain files to download, graphics, sound effects, or even video clips. You can browse the Web using AOL.

WWW *See* **World Wide Web**.

Smileys (Emoticons) and E-mail Abbreviations

One problem with e-mail messages is that there is no context in which to judge the words. Because e-mail can't convey tone of voice, facial expressions, body language, or even handwriting style, it can be hard to decipher the meaning of a message. Imagine that you had just done something unusual, and in response I sent you an e-mail message containing this sentence:

Good work!

Without any other cues, you might not be able to tell whether I was being sarcastic, angry, or congratulatory. That's where smileys and certain abbreviations come in. By adding these to e-mail messages, people can make clear what emotions go along with their words. Following are some of the most common emoticons and e-mail abbreviations.

Emoticons

NOTE   *To see the emoticons clearly, turn the paper to the right or tilt your head to the left.*

:-)   The basic smiley. It is used to show that you are smiling when you say whatever it is that precedes the smiley.

;-)   A winking smiley. Usually implies light sarcasm or a flirtatious remark. Kind of a "don't hit me for what I just said" smiley.

:-(A frowning smiley. The person who sent this either didn't like something that was just said or is upset/depressed about something.

:-I   An indifferent or apathetic smiley.

:->   Signifies a really sarcastic remark.

>:->   Signifies a devilish remark.

E-mail Abbreviations

AFAIK   As Far as I Know
BCNU   Be Seeing You

BTW	By the Way
FWIW	For What It's Worth
IIRC	If I Remember Correctly
IMHO	In My Humble Opinion
LOL	Laughing Out Loud
OBO	Or Best Offer
OTOH	On the Other Hand
ROTFL	Rolling on the Floor Laughing
RTFM	Read the F@#$ing Manual
TANSTAAFL	There Ain't No Such Thing as a Free Lunch
TTFN	Ta Ta for Now
TTYL	Talk to You Later

INDEX

ABOUT THE AUTHORS

Elizabeth Powell Crowe is the author of three books, including *Genealogy Online*, the previous editions of which were best-sellers. She also wrote *Information for Sale* (with John Everett) and *The Electronic Traveller*, both published by McGraw-Hill. She is the twice-monthly "Net Surfer" columnist for *Computer Currents* magazine and author of numerous articles for both popular and technical publications. She lives in Huntsville, Alabama, with her husband and two children.

Bill Mann is the author of seven books on diverse software, Internet, and online service books including *Politics on the Net*. He has written numerous articles on the Internet and on Internet-related topics. Bill resides in Bedford, New Hampshire.

Discover Just How Great Your Great, Great, Great Grandmother Really Was.

Introducing the **Ultimate Family™ Data Library** – the Ultimate standard in genealogy data.

Compiled and collected by nationally recognized genealogical professionals —
the Ultimate Family Data Library is your ticket to a rewarding journey into your family's past.
You might even be able to track down your great, great, great grandmother. And, since our Data CDs
are compatible with any genealogy software, quality data has never been easier to use.

■ **Easy to Find — Our Master Index has over 640,000 records.** Using our free Master Index you can search for an ancestor and determine which Data CDs from our library contain the detailed information. Visit the Master index at **www.familyinfo.com**

■ **Easy To Use — Viewer software included on all CDs.** We've made it easy. We have included the document viewer on each CD, so one CD is all you need. If you're a web user, you'll have free unlimited access to the Master Index. Plus, for a nominal subscription fee, you can have unlimited web access to all the data in our library.

AMERICA ONLINE *Exclusive!*

For a limited time, get the Social Security Death Index (SSDI) for only $9.95!*
(includes S & H)

With 55,000,000 names the SSDI lists everyone from the United States from 1920 to 1997 whose death benefits were claimed. This is a great place to start tracing your American family tree. To order mention code **DC11198**.

Expires June 30, 1999.

*Sales tax may be applicable

EASY TO ORDER!

To order or find out more about the Ultimate Family Data Library,

Phone: **1-888-891-1919**

E-mail: **ultimatedata@palladium.net**

Web: **www.familyinfo.com**

Order Code: DC11198

Ultimate Family Tree™

PALLADIUM INTERACTIVE®

Introducing the
AOL NETBOOK COLLECTION

The AOL Mouse Netbook

An innovative solution created exclusively for our members, this AOL MouseNetbook was designed to record and reference e-mail and web addresses quickly and easily. These convenient features include a comprehensive "glossary" of internet and technical terms and over 1,000 of AOL's most popular keywords. Customize your AOL MouseNetbook by inserting your favorite photos framed under the cover. The mousepad cover, made from Easy Track material, provides smooth movement and ease of control.

Item # 2817 $29.95

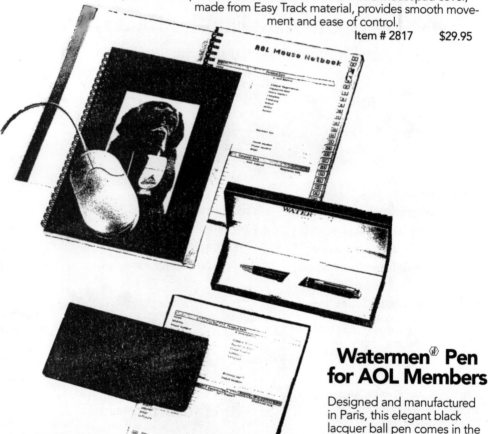

Watermen® Pen for AOL Members

Designed and manufactured in Paris, this elegant black lacquer ball pen comes in the Waterman signature blue box with white satin lining.

Item # 2807 $29.95

AOL Pocket Netbook

As the internet grows and becomes a larger part of your everyday life, so does the need for a quick and easy reference guide. This uniquely designed Netbook can be helpful for jotting down your favorite places online and recording names and addresses.

Item # 2809 $15.95

TO ORDER CALL: 1-800-844-3372 EXT. 1028

The Official AOL BOOK COLLECTION

America Online Official Guide to the Internet, 2nd Edition

The only guide to the Internet officially authorized by America Online. This new and updated 2nd edition has all the details on AOL's latest software-version 4.0 — written by David Peal, the former Editorial Manager of America Online's Internet Connection, this book explains how to use AOL's special navigational tools to find information fast and efficiently. It also explains how AOL makes accessing and using the Internet easy. Discover the Internet's possibilities as you learn how to plan a vacation, job hunt, make friends online and even create and post your own web site!

Item # 5532 $24.95

"David Peal draws on his years of working with AOL to share insider tips that can turn your Internet experience into something truly extraordinary" — Steve Case, Chairman and CEO of America Online.

World Wide Web Yellow Pages AOL Members Edition

This all-in-one guide to the World Wide Web, organized in familiar yellow pages format, helps you find the web sites you're looking for FAST. It contains detailed descriptions of over 10,000 sites, covering hundreds of subjects. A special introductory section, written exclusively for AOL members, explains how to navigate the WWW and the Internet quickly and expertly! The BONUS searchable CD-ROM is an electronic version of the book that lets you click on sites and travel the web hassle free!

Item # 5517 $34.99

The America Online Insider's Guide to Finding Information Online

AOL experts share the ins and outs of finding information online by explaining how to approach a search. From locating business and personal contacts, to tracking down facts, to accessing rare texts, this book helps you develop your own powers of discovery. Learn to use AOL's powerful search tools — like AOL NetFind, Find, Channel search options, and Keywords — to find the information you want—at the click of a mouse. Plus tips and ideas for searching the 50 most popular topics online. The trick is knowing where you want to go - this book will show you how to get there! From AOL Press.

Item # 5469 $24.95

TO ORDER CALL: 1-800-844-3372 EXT. 1028

The Official AOL BOOK COLLECTION

America Online Tour Guide, Version 4.0

The definitive guide for AOL members since its first edition in 1992. This all-new edition covers all the exciting, new, timesaving, fun features of AOL's latest release, AOL 4.0! Your personal tourguide to AOL, it takes you through the basics, then helps you advance, by explaining some of more powerful features that are built into the service. The original AOL guide, author Tom Lichty has helped more than 1 million AOL members get started. You'll appreciate his engaging and humorous style. Over 600 pages - everything you need to know to enhance your online experience with AOL. For both Windows and Macintosh users.

Item # 5053 $24.95

The Official America Online Yellow Pages

Want to find a particular area on AOL but don't have much time to search? Then let the all new Official America Online Yellow Pages help you find what you are looking for instantly! This complete guide covers thousands of AOL sites, providing full descriptions and keywords. It makes accessing news, stock quotes, sports stats, and even the latest entertainment scoop, as easy as typing in one word. Organized in Yellow Pages style, it will save you time & money by helping you find what you want on AOL fast!

Item # 5468 $24.95

The Insider's Guide to America Online

AOL's own Meg has written the first true Insider's guide to America Online. Experienced AOLers know Meg as the author of all the cool Inside tips at Keyword: Insider. In this book, Meg has compiled and organized those great tips to give you the inside scoop on AOL: the BEST areas and the most USEFUL tools. Learn how to manage your personal finances and investments online, find bargains on everything from flowers to automobiles, locate the best areas for kids and families, find the lowest airfares and best travel deals…and much more.

Item # 5461 $24.95

Upgrade & Repair Your PC
on a Shoestring - AOL Members Edition

Suffering from new computer envy? Well don't throw that old computer away just yet! This book provides the solid advice and information you need to make your computer run faster and do the things you want without a Ph.D. in Computer Technology and a boatload of money! Four sections talk you through upgrading your PC with lots of friendly advice and encouragement. From determining what you need, to explaining components and what they do, to the Nuts & Bolts with complete illustrations and instructions, to resources on AOL to help you through the process. This book also features the information you need to troubleshoot and make simple repairs yourself. Written in simple, easy to understand language for all computer users .

Item # 5055 $24.95

TO ORDER CALL: 1-800-844-3372 EXT. 1028

GRAPHICS MADE FUN AND EASY
for the whole family!

AOL Member Exclusive!

For Windows 95 and Windows 3.1

AMERICA ONLINE's GRAPHICSuite

Excellent for Home, School or Business

Enter the exciting world of digital imaging - no experience necessary!

America Online's GraphicSuite

Now you can produce professional-looking art on your computer even if you've never worked with digital art before. Our AOL exclusive GraphicSuite CD-Rom makes it easy! Ten top-rated, user friendly programs on one CD-ROM give you the tools to create, retouch, and organize images, then import them into your documents or post them on a Web site.

✔ Turn ordinary photos into dazzling banners, greeting cards and more!

✔ Add animation and sound to your e-mail!

✔ Organize your images with drag and drop ease!

✔ 10,000 ready-to-use clip art photos and images! **BONUS**

Item # 6708 - $29.95

TO ORDER CALL: 1-800-844-3372 EXT. 1028

Energize your AOL & INTERNET EXPERIENCE

NEW!

Start getting more from AOL and the Internet today!

AOL's Internet AcceleratorSuite

Improve your computer's performance and speed up your Web access with AOL's exclusive Internet AcceleratorSuite! Contains over 12 top-selling titles on one CD-ROM to optimize your Internet experience! Create exciting Web sites, protect your computer from viruses and keep your kids safe on the Internet!

- ✔ Launch to a Web site with a single keystroke!
- ✔ Create a Web page in as little as 15 minutes!
- ✔ Detect and eliminate connection problems!
- ✔ Add animation, sound and clip art to your Web site!

Item # 6748 - $39.95

TO ORDER CALL: 1-800-844-3372 EXT. 1028

Order your Books, CD-ROMs and AOL Netbook Collections Today

To order by phone: **1-800-884-3372**, ext. 1028
To order by fax: 1-800-827-4595

Item #	Title	Quantity	Unit Price	Total Price
5532	AOL Official Guide the Internet, 2nd Edition		$24.95	
5517	World Wide Web Yellow Pages AOL Edition		$34.99	
5469	AOL Insider's Guide to Finding Information Online		$24.95	
5053	America Online Tour Guide, Version 4.0		$24.95	
5468	The Official America Online Yellow Pages		$24.95	
5461	The Insider's Guide to America Online		$24.95	
5055	Upgrade & Repair Your PC on a Shoestring		$24.95	
6550	America Online's PowerSuite		$29.95	
6708	America Online's GraphicSuite		$29.95	
6748	AOL's Internet AcceleratorSuite		$39.95	
2817	The AOL Mouse Netbook		$29.95	
2807	Watermen Pen for AOL Members		$29.95	
2809	AOL Pocket Netbook		$15.95	

Prices subject to change without notice.

Shipping and Handling:
Under $20.00 = $4.00
$21.00 - $30.00 = $4.25
$31.00 - 40.00 = $4.75
Over $50.00 = $5.00

Subtotal $ ——————
Shipping & Handling $ ——————
Sales Tax may be applicable $ ——————
Total $ ——————

ORDERED BY:

Name ————————————————

Address————————————————

City/State/Zip Code ——————————

Daytime Phone Number (___) ———— - ————

SHIP TO: (if different from above)

Name ————————————————

Address————————————————

City/State/Zip Code ——————————

Daytime Phone Number (___) ———— - ————

METHOD OF PAYMENT
☐ VISA
☐ MasterCard
☐ Discover
☐ American Express

☐☐☐☐☐☐☐☐☐☐☐☐☐☐☐☐☐
Account Number

Expiration Date: ☐☐ - ☐☐

————————————————
Signature
(Required for all credit card orders)

Send order form and payment to:
America Online, Inc.
Department 1028
P.O. Box 2530
Kearneysville, WV 25430-9935

BB28